Quests of Difference

Quests of Difference:
Reading Pope's Poems

G. Douglas Atkins

THE UNIVERSITY PRESS OF KENTUCKY

Scholarly publisher for the Commonwealth, serving Bellarmine College, Berea
College, Centre College of Kentucky, Eastern Kentucky University, The Filson
Club, Georgetown College, Kentucky Historical Society, Kentucky State Uni-
versity, Morehead State University, Murray State University, Northern Kentucky
University, Transylvania University, University of Kentucky, University of Louis-
ville, and Western Kentucky University.

Editorial and Sales Offices: Lexington, Kentucky 40506–0024

Library of Congress Cataloging-in-Publication Data

Atkins, G. Douglas (George Douglas), 1943–
 Quests of difference.

 Bibliography: p.
 Includes index.
  1. Pope, Alexander, 1688–1744—Criticism and
interpretation. 2. Deconstruction. I. Title.
PR3634.A85 1986   821'.5   85-20228
ISBN 0-8131-1565-5

For my relatives

Contents

Preface

This study of Pope's poems, an exercise in what I call reader-responsibility criticism, consists of readings of individual texts, rather than a single argument concerning them. Before the latter can be done (assuming that it is desirable), the texts must be read, and reading entails the complex and demanding work that I try to describe in my first chapter. What I offer here is a series of essays planned as a book. The essays are frankly exploratory and tentative, and they make no pretense of definitiveness.

Nor have I tried in any sense to be complete in my treatment of Pope's poems. I do not, for example, claim to read all the major poems. In this regard, the most glaring omission is probably *The Rape of the Lock*. One important reason for not including an essay on it is that I have preferred to treat Pope's own essayistic and more intellectual poems. Accordingly, in reading *The Dunciad* I concentrate on the fourth book, and though I consider many of the Horatian satires, I focus on the essays and epistles. This procedure results in a certain lack of balance, since I write about one poem in each of three chapters, several poems in each of two others. The differential treatment given the various poems is, I believe, consonant with their nature and their respective importance.

The essayistic nature of my efforts, it is only fair to point out, entails a certain amount of repetition, at least some of which signals the lack of any straight-line development or progression in Pope's writing. His texts frequently repeat points, as he swerves back, covering ground already explored. Not only does he completely overhaul *The Dunciad,* but the later version is itself an inversion of *An Essay on Man,* the concerns and strategies of which also appear in the *Moral Essays.* A less essayistic, and more argumentative, mode would risk both obscuring the similarities and flattening out the differences involved in these returns, perhaps positing a progression that in Pope is fitful at best. Pope's poems do display many important recurring concerns, some of which I focus on, but we should be wary of too easily assuming that, "correctly understood," they form a clear and definite progression.

I do not mean to breathe new life into the notion that Pope is, despite brilliant flashes, an uneven writer or an inconsistent and naively contradictory thinker. *An Essay on Man,* in particular, has proved to be fertile ground for those bent on discrediting "the wasp of Twickenham" by holding up for condemnation the apparent self-contradictions. Blunders there may well be, in this poem as well as others. I have no interest in either excusing Pope or trying to rescue him from his detractors by denying the force of their criticism. My interest is different: I stress the heterogeneity of Pope's (and all other) discourse, accepting it and regarding at least much of it as a signifying structure that we will do well to attend to.

Though interested in the relations among Pope's poems, the relation of poem to poem (a point that he himself stresses), I resist the perhaps natural impulse to look for and expect a neat and coherent whole, whether reading a single text or a group of texts, such as the *Moral Essays.* Along with Jacques Derrida, Geoffrey Hartman, and others, I prefer to open rather than to close poems—another reason for choosing the essay form for these studies. The whole we almost inevitably seek turns out to have a hole in it.

My procedure throughout involves bringing together Pope's poems and the interests of contemporary critical theory, especially deconstruction, and exploring their relations, without positing the latter as the long-sought key that will unlock the secrets of Pope's artistry. As a matter of fact, I suggest that as a mode of close reading deconstruction lacks responsibility unless it includes, as a first "phase," attention to authorial declarations, which it proceeds to situate. Such double reading as I describe in the first chapter by no means excludes traditional questions concerning critical tact, it is not exempt from Pope's surely right injunction to read sympathetically and generously, and it certainly does nothing to minimize the reader's obligations to be informed, rigorous, and scrupulous.

Moreover, in Chapters Two through Six, I do not so much apply deconstruction as a method for reading texts as read Pope in light of deconstruction. As it happens, I wrote the first chapter, explaining the principles of double reading, only after completing the readings of Pope's poems. In at least one sense, therefore, the readings precede the theory. The relation of strategy to reading, theory to practice, is, then, not a simple one. To describe the relation of deconstructive strategy to the readings that follow, I can think (appropriately enough) of no better account than Pope's own in writing of the relation of *An Essay on Man* to the remainder of the projected "ethic" poems. That is, adapting Pope's terms from "The Design" of his theodicy, I might say that the principles of what I call double reading provide a general map, marking out the territory, offering a sense of direction, but leaving the particulars to be "delineated" as we attend closely to the topography that is Pope's poems. What Pope adds, I repeat: in the first chapter "I am . . . only opening the *fountains*, and clearing the passage. To deduce the *rivers*, to follow them in their course, and to observe their effects" is the task of the succeeding chapters.

One other point concerning my strategies and procedures here, which has to do with the essayistic nature of the chapters: I regard the critical essay as more than a medium for the elucidation of other texts. It has, or should have, value in its own right as an art form (I esteem the possibilities of the form, not my execution of them). At the same time, elucidation of the texts that have occasioned it remains a crucial function of the critical essay, and I have tried both to shed some light on Pope's poems and to direct attention to a way of reading and responding that will prove productive (rather than authoritative).

I should comment, finally, on the tone and style of these essays. As the relatively small number of references to the rich and illuminating commentary on Pope may imply, I have written not just for the "professional Popean." I have written as well for that elusive (and perhaps illusive) general reader that all commentators hope to interest. Whether or not either type of reader will approve, I have tried not to take my treatment of the subject too seriously (I like to think that Pope would approve). Thus the tone is sometimes light and playful. That difference from most of the scholarship on Pope* may suggest that the quests in my title allude to my own desires as well as refer to Pope's. In any case, the question of the "proper" is raised: What is the reader's "proper" stance before poems encountered?

---

*My discussion is related to—different from but certainly indebted to—Maynard Mack's "On Reading Pope" (*College English*, 7 [1946], 263-73) and George S. Rousseau's "On Reading Pope" (in *Alexander Pope*, ed. Peter Dixon [Athens: Ohio Univ. Press, 1972], pp. 1-59).

What sort of "answerable style" is "proper"? As I have already suggested, the issue of critical tact is unavoidable, and in developing my response to reading Pope I have tried to be temperate as well as responsible.

The debts I have incurred in making this study are many. First of all, I want to thank three (somewhat different) teachers and mentors, to whom all readers of Pope are mightily indebted: the late Irvin Ehrenpreis, Maynard Mack, and Aubrey Williams. If there is a *genius loci* of the essays, it is probably Geoffrey Hartman, whose generous encouragement and support of this project and others it is a pleasure to acknowledge. I want to thank, too, Joel Weinsheimer, especially for invitations to speak and to write on *Bathurst*. I do not imply that any of these critics would accept my readings or positions. Without the good offices of Sandee Kennedy, I might well still be typing the first draft of the second chapter; graciously, with amazing patience and consummate skill and efficiency, she transcribed my hieroglyphical handwriting onto an ATMS. Without the personal and professional support of my former chairman, Gerhard Zuther, my labors would have been harder, my life far more difficult. Finally, I gratefully acknowledge the continuing support of the University of Kansas, especially for summer grants through the General Research Fund and for a sabbatical leave, during which most of the writing was completed.

My discussion of *Sober Advice from Horace* draws on material that first appeared in *Papers on Language & Literature* 15 (1979): 159–74; and my discussion of *An Epistle to Bathurst* is a revised version of an essay published in *The Eighteenth Century: Theory and Interpretation* 24 (1983): 65–78. I am grateful to the editors for permission to incorporate this material here. An earlier version of my discussion of *An Epistle to Dr. Arbuthnot* appeared in my book *Reading Deconstruction/Deconstructive Reading* (University Press of Kentucky, 1983).

A note on the text: Throughout I have used, and quoted from, the Twickenham Edition of *The Poems of Alexander Pope*, ed. John Butt et al., 11 vols. (New Haven: Yale Univ. Press, and London: Methuen, 1939-69).

Quests of Difference

~ Chapter One

Double Reading Pope

Several years ago I wrote an essay on Pope and Deism that I hoped would be a prolegomenon to a study of the poet's religious positions.[1] That discussion, in which I concluded that it is "highly improbable" that Pope ever was, like his good friend Bolingbroke, a Deist, received some attention, and the positive response encouraged me to go beyond saying what Pope was not to (I hoped) an eventual definitive statement concerning what he was, religiously. For years I dutifully tried to pinpoint what is peculiar to Christianity, Deism, and Catholicism; to sort out the Christian and the perhaps Deistic strains in Pope's thinking; and to distinguish the Catholic from the non-Catholic elements as well as the Erasmian Catholic from the Thomistic. My goal was to resolve the dispute concerning Pope's apparently equivocal position on matters religious, to settle once and for all questions regarding his faith. I thus tried to make some absolute distinctions concerning Pope's religious thinking—even though I could not (and still cannot) draw such clear and definite lines between differences in my own thinking.

Though the difficulty of the task I set for myself was considerable, I persevered, my efforts revolving about the only "unwobbling pivot" I was ever able to locate, Pope's determined and pervasive anti-sectarianism and the parts-whole figure that structures it and so many other aspects of his writing. I persevered, that is, until I began reading critical theory, eventually becoming a practitioner of (and an occasional apologist for) deconstruction, variously depicted as "degenerate criticism," a form of "hermeneutical high-jinks," and a sophisticated mode of close reading having enormous potential for changing—for the better—the way we regard all texts, human and social as well as graphic. It was just this "affirmative" nature that attracted me to deconstruction. And though, as I have argued elsewhere,[2] deconstruction certainly prizes historical and scholarly research, building on it rather than ignoring or rejecting it, it did bring in its wake—at least for me—a new set of attitudes, priorities, and goals.

With regard to my specific interests in Pope, three points emerged clearly. First, like Paul de Man, who writes in *Allegories of Reading* that he "began to read Rousseau seriously in preparation for a historical reflection on Romanticism" only to find himself "unable to progress beyond local difficulties of interpretation,"[3] I gradually realized that I could say nothing about Pope's religious positions until I had more carefully *read* his texts (the correspondence as well as the poetry, the former requiring interpretation no less than the latter). Complex, difficult, and equivocal, these texts demand the most scrupulous attention. Second, after learning to read more closely and rigorously than I had before, and then beginning to read Pope with some of the care that he devoted to the writing of his texts, I came reluctantly to regard many questions concerning his religious positions as neither very interesting nor particularly important, especially as they tend to reduce to narrow doctrinal and institutional considerations. The search is often for what Prufrock calls "a formulated phrase" by which the poet, a particularly intriguing specimen, is "pinned and wriggling on the wall" for all to observe and to judge. Finally, I realized, as my interests shifted toward language, that in reading we are always in the "presence" of religious and theological concerns, even if they are not thematized or explicitly stated. This is so because, as Derrida maintains, "the age of the sign is essentially theological": "the intelligible face of the sign remains turned toward the word and the face of God."[4] It may be that what language has to "say" about God and religious questions will turn out to be at least as interesting and important as the declarations we make. In order to find out, we have to read.

We thus return to my first, apparently unexceptionable point, which deserves some clarification. Surely no one would dispute that we must carefully *read* a writer's texts before attempting an interpretation of his or her intellectual, political, or religious positions, but, as I have hinted by italicizing the word, I mean something quite specific by the term *reading*. First of all, my sense is akin to what de Man describes as "genuinely analytical reading," which he distinguishes from paraphrase, "the mainstay of all critical reading." Whereas, de Man asserts, the purpose of paraphrase "is to blur, confound, and hide discontinuities and disruptions in the homogeneity of its own discourse," paralleling the author's efforts to conceal and divert "what stands in the way of his own meaning," the reading this critic solicits "would no longer blindly submit to the teleology of controlled meaning."[5] De Man thus calls for a reading that refuses to rest satisfied with an elucidating account of an author's meaning but goes on, reading "against the grain" (that is, in my formulation, against the explicit declarations) and so producing the text's deconstruction.

For de Man, reading "has to go against the grain of what one would want to happen in the name of what has to happen."[6] In the following paragraphs, I turn the figure somewhat differently, and the particular turn I give to de Man's formulation suggests that I am describing one particular approach to a general position or movement and so justifies, I believe, my covering again some territory that is increasingly known to a wide range of readers. Though I think it faithful to basic principles and strategies of deconstruction, and certainly in line with the exposition I offered in a recent book,[7] the position I take places emphasis, highlights points, and works out strategies that other deconstructionists might quarrel with. Derridean deconstruction is not de Manian deconstruction, and many deconstructionists, of whatever "school," may resist my particular insistence on reading with and against the grain, which is an abstraction from and a schematization of a textual field that in fact is richly integumented. Suffice it to say here that the shape given to deconstructive strategies in these pages derives from my understanding of deconstruction as an affirmative and eminently practical (as well as impure) activity with important implications for our ethical and social lives.

Whatever their exact contours, the positions that I and others (somewhat differently) name deconstruction are often misunderstood. For many, the refusal to "submit to the teleology of controlled meaning" is tantamount to opening the floodgates, welcoming subjectivism and even solipsism, and allowing the reader to determine meaning. Anarchy is supposedly loosed, as anything goes and a sophomore's dilated meaning is just as good as the distinguished scholar's. Such a reading of de Man's account, however, grossly misrepresents what he calls for. What many fail (or prefer not) to see is that the refusal to "submit to the teleology of controlled meaning" need not involve neglect or ignorance of authorial meaning. Rather than subjectivism or irresponsibility, deconstruction (at least as it is practiced in impure form by a critic like Geoffrey Hartman) may more properly be considered a type of what I call *reader-responsibility*, a term that both avoids any suggestion of aesthetic distance and in fact implies the "call" and the "burden" placed on the reader to keep texts alive and to respond in meaningful ways to the possibilities opened up.[8] At any rate, you can't deliberately read against the grain until you know the grain.

Derrida makes essentially the same point, writing in *Of Grammatology* that "reading must always aim at a certain relationship, unperceived by the writer, between what he commands and what he does not command of the patterns of the language that he uses."[9] That an author, no matter how skillful and meticulous, is never fully in control of his or her language results from many factors, important among them being what Geoffrey Hartman calls "the equivocal character of words."[10] Derrida goes on to spell out the necessity of employing traditional interpretive procedures: without "all the instruments of traditional criticism . . . critical production would risk developing in any direction at all and authorize itself to say almost anything. But this indispensable guardrail has always only *protected*, it has never *opened*, a reading."[11] Though some deconstructionists apparently prefer to think otherwise, proudly announcing "the death of the author," Derrida insists that "the category of intention will not disappear." He adds, however, that though "it will have its place, . . . from this place it will no longer be able to govern the entire scene and the entire system of utterances."[12] Intention, in other words, is to be *situated*. Like de Man, then, Derrida thus advocates a kind of double reading, and, according to Derrida, that reading consists of a relationship that "is not a certain quantitative distribution of shadow and light, of weakness or of force, but a signifying structure that critical reading should *produce.*" [13]

One must first, therefore, attend to what Derrida, in *Of Grammatology*, calls the text's *declarations:* its explicit meanings, more or less coinciding with the author's apparent intentions. This constructive "step" or "phase" [14] tries to get inside a text to determine, among other things, how it is made; it considers both meanings and the enabling conditions that allow meanings to be produced. Pope's point in *An Essay on Criticism* is of immense value in this initial "phase" of reading: he insists that we read a text "With the same Spirit that its Author *writ*" (l. 234). But having thus followed the grain, one goes on, not being bound (as Pope suggests) by authorially controlled meanings, to "open" a reading. Thus defined, reading consists of attending to both what an author "commands and what he does not command of the patterns of the language that he uses" (I follow Derrida in calling the latter the text's *descriptions*). Only this both/and process, I would argue, exercises reader-responsibility, attending to intention but, rather than being limited to it, proceeding to situate it in a discourse that it no longer dominates. The two "steps" or "phases" of this both/and process exist in tension, neither dominating or controlling the other. It is not, then, that reading against the grain comes to replace the declared or intentional meanings. Is a neglect of textual descriptions any less irresponsible than a neglect of authorial declarations?

Though it is only in the past twenty years or so that we seem to have been particularly concerned with what exceeds a writer's conscious grasp and control, these "descriptions" are hardly less important than the author's declarations, and they tell their story in all texts, no matter the writer or the period. To understand exactly how textual descriptions come about, let us turn—briefly—to Derrida's accounts of the production of slippage in language and of the linguistic excess that a writer, no matter how careful, is unable to control. Derrida uses several closely related terms in treating this (rather humbling) situation, whereby mastery eludes us. Among these terms are *différance* and the "trace." He extends Saussure's seminal analysis of the differential character of language ("In language," according to the linguist, "there are only differences, *without positive terms*"),[15] coining the term *différance* to describe what in *Positions* he calls "the systematic play of differences, of the traces of differences, of the *spacing* by means of which elements are related to each other. This spacing is the simultaneously active and passive (the *a* of *différance* indicates this indecision as concerns activity and passivity, that which cannot be governed by or distributed between the terms of this opposition) production of the intervals without which the 'full' terms would not signify, would not function."[16] Indeed, Derrida shows that "Differance is what makes the movement of signification possible":[17] "Without a retention in the minimal unit of temporal experience, without a trace retaining the other as other in the same, no difference would do its work and no meaning would appear. It is not the question of a constituted difference here, but rather, before all determination of the content, of the *pure* movement which produces difference. *The (pure) trace is differance.*"[18]

A notion cognate to *différance*, and particularly important to an understanding of Pope, is supplementarity. In a section of the *Grammatology* entitled "That Dangerous Supplement," Derrida explains its strange logic:

The supplement adds itself, it is a surplus, a plenitude enriching another plenitude, the *fullest measure* of presence. It cumulates and accumulates presence. It is thus that art, *technè*, image, representation, convention, etc., come as supplements to nature and are rich with this entire cumulating function. . . .
  But the supplement supplements. It adds only to replace. It intervenes or insinuates itself *in-the-place-of;* if it fills, it is as if one fills a void. If it represents and makes an image, it is by the anterior default of a presence.[19]

As Barbara Johnson has written, Derrida's analysis of supplementarity, in exemplary readings of its production in *Of Grammatology* and *Dissemination,* is "nothing less than a revolution in the very logic of meaning." She explains:

The logic of the supplement wrenches apart the neatness of the metaphysical binary oppositions. Instead of "A is opposed to B" we have "B is both added to A and replaces A." A and B are no longer opposed, nor are they equivalent. Indeed, they are no longer even equivalent to themselves. They are their own difference from themselves. "Writing," for example, no longer means simply "words on a page," but rather any differential trace structure. . . . "Writing" and "speech" [for example] can therefore no longer be simply opposed, but neither have they become identical. Rather, the very notion of their "identities" is put in question.

As a result, Johnson writes, the supplement "carries the text's signifying possibilities beyond what could reasonably be attributed to [an author's] conscious intentions."[20]
  Supplementarity thus produces what exceeds conscious intention, what goes beyond authorially controlled meaning. This excess has, in fact, a particular character and effect, resulting in a textual description that *wars* with authorial declaration. Involved, moreover, is something other

and greater than local contradictions—a point particu-
larly important in considering Pope, who has frequently
been charged with inconsistency and self-contradiction.
To quote Barbara Johnson again, "Derrida's reading
shows how Rousseau's text functions *against* its own ex-
plicit (metaphysical) assertions, not just by creating am-
biguity, but by inscribing a *systematic* 'other message' be-
hind or through what is being said."[21] Texts thus are
divided within, differing from "themselves," and that self-
difference is a matter, not of an isolated inconsistency,
contradiction, or error, but of a *systematic* narrative or
story being told that undermines the more or less explicit
declarations.

That internal division "wrenches apart" all oppositions,
including the apparent opposition I have just posited be-
tween authorial declaration and textual description. Rob-
ert Magliola has recently accused J. Hillis Miller of un-
wittingly lapsing into just such logocentrism when he
"organizes his criticism as constructive (the positing of a
monologic reading) and deconstructive (the subversion of
this reading)." Produced, claims Magliola, "is a closed
pattern structured as a formal opposition."[22] Whether or
not this pattern actually occurs in Miller's practice,[23] it is
not inherent in deconstructive criticism. The supplement
produces a both/and situation, supposed oppositions
being revealed as "their own differance from themselves."
What this means in the case of declaration/description is
that each term is already divided within, the monologic
reading already containing within it its own deconstruc-
tion, just as the deconstruction contains the monologic in-
side it; that (therefore) there is a ceaseless oscillation be-
tween the two readings, each being deconstructible in
terms of the other; and that the reader is unable to decide
between them, to determine the priority of the one over
the other.

Further, the systematic description written through what is being declared does not result from the willful imposition by the reader of a theory or meaning "extrinsic" to the text. Contrary to the allegations of opponents of such double reading, the "*systematic* 'other message'" is *there*, in the textual description—though it requires the work of the reader for its story to be "heard." The reader is thus actively involved, helping to present that story and being, as Roland Barthes claims, "no longer a consumer, but a producer of the text."[24] The reader-text relation is another both/and situation: despite the claims of both objectivists and subjectivists, the former privileging the text just as the latter make the reader determiner of meaning, both reader and text are involved in a story of struggle for mastery.[25]

This way of understanding reading as the story of the ineluctable involvement of both reader and text seems especially suitable in the case of Pope. It may at last allow us to bring the reader into the study of Pope's poetry, from which he or she has heretofore largely been excluded. I by no means wish to deny or minimize the contributions of work produced under the powerful influence of New Criticism, which in one form or another has dominated Pope studies for decades, but increasingly we are aware of the price paid for those notable achievements. Certainly the flesh-and-blood reader, in a specific historical situation with a panoply of desires, has mattered little (or so it has been assumed and argued) in the determination of poetic meaning. Frederick M. Keener maintains that the twentieth-century reader of Pope has by and large effaced himself or herself before the poems: "Elegant, aloof, most modern criticism of Pope reads as if it emanated not from twentieth-century America or England but from some miraculously undisturbed eighteenth-century estate, what

Hugh Kenner has called 'the professional Popeans' Natchez-Augustan manor'"; the goal, according to Keener, has been to read Pope's poems as if one were his "ideal contemporary": "the critic becomes a chameleon on the poetry, bringing out color but himself disappearing in the process."[26] Certainly Pope studies would benefit, as would some more austere forms of deconstruction, from Geoffrey Hartman's insistence on the chiasmic relationship of critic and text, a situation, indeed, of interrelationship in which texts receive their strength from the strength they give.[27] In relating Pope and theory, and in shuttling between Pope's poetry and the formal ideas of recent critical theory, I have tried in these essays to keep Hartman's teaching in mind, though I grant the limitations of my effort as well as the need (unfulfilled here) to consider the relationship of Pope's texts and their readers in light of work currently being advanced by the so-called new historicism.

At any rate, deconstruction holds out the possibility, not only of correcting the situation Keener laments and bringing the reader and his or her historically situated interests (for example, interest in deconstruction) into the interpretive process, but also of considering other neglected concerns. One of the several opportunities deconstruction offers the student of Pope is precisely the consideration of concerns and strategies largely unremarked. Among them, as it happens, are Pope's ways of involving and implicating the reader in the production of his meanings (about which more shortly) and his not-infrequent way of both de-mythologizing and even deconstructing. De-mythologizing occurs prominently in *An Essay on Man* as Pope shatters various myths concerning man and his capacities, and deconstruction appears in, for example, the *Epistle to Burlington* as Pope describes Bubo's mansion as a "standing sermon" against "Magnificence" (ll. 19-22).

What Pope does here, and elsewhere, parallels what deconstruction involves: he reads against the grain. In the chapters that follow, I explore various relations Pope's poetry has with deconstruction. Deconstruction exists within Pope's poems in at least three ways: like other texts, Pope's deconstruct themselves; Pope sometimes adopts positions and offers statements that, as in *Burlington*, clearly parallel deconstruction; and such a poem as *Dunciad* IV offers an intriguing twist by providing the occasion to read deconstruction in light of Pope.[28]

Far from entailing an imposition of theory or of the reader's desires on (helpless) texts, deconstruction actually shares with Pope some fundamental attitudes and strategies. One central concern of deconstruction—difference—is also, in its many forms, one of Pope's major concerns. Focusing on difference, as I will do in this book, is, then, a way of being faithful both to Pope's apparent intentions and to the strategy of reading that I believe currently offers the deepest and richest "approach" to texts.

Difference is, first of all, a prominent fact about Pope's life. He was *different:* Roman Catholic in an Anglican country, unusually short, hunchbacked, prone to disease (in *An Epistle to Dr. Arbuthnot*, he writes movingly of "this long Disease, my Life," l. 132), acutely sensitive, and greatly talented—these and other well-rehearsed facts contributed to Pope's difference. However, and to whatever degree, his personal difference affected his writing, Pope's poems in various ways involve quest(ion)s of difference: for example, a desire of personal distinction and differentiation, efforts on behalf of cultural discrimination, and attempts to preserve and enhance social and political order. In the poetry difference functions not merely as both a major theme and a goal but also as an important strategy involving the reader. A number of Pope's poems are so constructed as to call into play, test, and increase the reader's ability to make certain necessary distinctions and discriminations. No matter the particular operation of difference, apparent throughout Pope's poetry is a determined opposition to equivocation (in *Arbuthnot* he reserves his severest criticism for Sporus, "one vile Antithesis. / Amphibious Thing!" [ll. 325-26]).

Characteristic of Pope, in fact, is a quest of clear, distinct lines and absolute differences. Typically structured around binary oppositions, Pope's poems explore relations between inside and outside, proper and improper, truth and un-truth, reading and writing, self and other. Pope's declared position generally is that the difference between the terms in such oppositions can be determined and stated unequivocally. Like that of the "theoretical" man in Nietzsche's *The Birth of Tragedy*, Pope's appears to be the "unshakable faith that thought, using the thread of logic," can "separate true knowledge from appearance and error." [29] No matter how fine it is, and no matter the difficulty we have in perceiving it, there is always for Pope what *An Essay on Man* calls "th' insuperable line" (I. 228), establishing difference.

That contemporary critical theory shares Pope's interest in and work with difference should already be apparent from my discussion above of deconstruction. In fact, there is a "tradition of difference," which J. Hillis Miller has described in a review essay on M. H. Abrams's *Natural Supernaturalism*. Obviously indebted to Saussure, this tradition maintains that difference, rather than identity or sameness, is originary: "similarity arises from difference rather than difference from similarity." I quote from Miller's important elaboration on this point:

The situation of dispersal, separation, and unappeasable desire is the "original" and perpetual human predicament. The dream of primal and final unity, always deferred, never present here and now, is generated by the original and originating differentiation. The beginning was diacritical.

Such an alternative pattern to the one Abrams traces would deny that the One comes first. It would deny the existence of "opposites" which are fragmented parts of an original whole. It would deny that history has a goal of reunification. In place of the notion that the origin is unity, Nietzsche, Deleuze, or Derrida would put the idea of a primal difference or differentiation. . . . In place of the notion of opposites ("Without contraries is no progression," said Blake), Nietzsche would put the idea of degrees of difference, differentiated forces which are not opposites, but points on the same scale, distinctions of the same energy, as reason is nature deferred or separated from itself. "There are no more opposites:" wrote Nietzsche, "only from those of logic do we derive the concept of opposites—and falsely transfer it to things."

Even that most stable notion of univocity and identity, the self, is deconstructed by the "tradition of difference," as Miller explains: "In place of the notion of the unity of the thinking subjectivity so essential to the project of the humanization of metaphysics, Nietzsche would put the idea of a multiplicity of forces struggling for dominion within the 'self': 'The assumption of one single subject is perhaps unnecessary; perhaps it is just as permissible to assume a multiplicity of subjects, whose interaction and struggle is the basis of our thought and our consciousness in general? A kind of aristocracy of equals, used to ruling jointly and understanding how to command?/*My hypothesis:* The subject as multiplicity.'" Miller points out that "this alternative scheme, with its various aspects or motifs, has always been present as a shadow or reversed mirror image within the Western tradition."[30] To reveal its operation in Pope's poems, and to narrate the story it produces there, is a major goal of this book, which might be considered an extended meditation on Miller's account of the "tradition of difference."

But even if a "tradition of difference" must be rigorously distinguished from a "tradition of identity,"[31] common sense alone suggests that sameness and difference do not and cannot exist in the other's absence, indeed that they have no meaning apart from each other. They are, therefore, *always already* related, and that relational structure owes nothing to man and his efforts. *Différance* names the structure wherein sameness is inhabited by—contains a "trace" of—difference, just as difference is inhabited by and contains a "trace" of sameness. Relation thus derives from *différance*, rather than from human effort: because entities (linguistic, social, human) differ not only from one another (though not absolutely) but also from "themselves," differences between them are mitigated, and, there being no absolutely distinct, univocal identities, relation exists. It is available to us (like—or as—grace?) if only we will accept it. Pope's poems tell this story.

Chapter Two

Fair Art's "Treach'rous Colours"

The Fate of "Gen'rous Converse" *in* An Essay on Criticism

How better to begin a critical reading of Pope's poems than by attending to what he writes about reading? Though he thematizes reading most prominently in the moral epistles and satires of the 1730s, Pope's first major poem, *An Essay on Criticism*, already offers clear insight into a range of related issues. Here Pope treats not only reading but also language, the relation of language to thought, the relation of readers to texts, and much more. In discussing the *Essay*, I shall focus on this matter of relations, particularly the kinds of relation obtaining within the various differences that serve to structure the poem.

On Reading Generously

The remarkably rich commentary published on *An Essay on Criticism* both provides the occasion and prompts the desire to reread it. I begin with one of the strongest recent readings of the *Essay*, that by David B. Morris. Entitled "Civilized Reading: The Act of Judgment in *An Essay on Criticism*," this study is important not only for its carefully considered argument that Pope's poem merits a place of some distinction in the history of literary theory but also for its own sensitive—and civilized—analysis of the poem as poem.[1] As he perceptively focuses on the role of generosity in the poem and in the theory it elaborates, Morris reminds us of Pope's important use of the parts-whole problem,[2] particularly in directing attention to the reader-text relationship thematized in *An Essay on Criticism.* Though he does not develop the point, Morris suggests that the poem, in discussing the act of reading, tells us how it itself is to be read.

Morris's account runs somewhat as follows: Interpreting pride as the virtual opposite of the generosity Pope advocates, Morris claims that the "effect of pride, within the context of Pope's *Essay*, is always a pressure toward partiality and fragmentation, blocking comprehensiveness of vision. In its pressure against wholeness, pride radically constricts understanding by attaching us to cherished opinions and to favored fragments."[3] Generosity plays the hero to the villain pride in this critical story, permitting the necessary attention to the whole. It makes possible "an equitable judgment by consciously rejecting whatever is incomplete and partisan."[4] Questions remain, however, as Morris recognizes. How, he asks,

can the critic gain access to the author's mental processes and undeclared purposes which are required for understanding the "*Whole*" work? Pope's answer to this difficult question is the power of sympathy. Sympathy, like friendship and virtue, is a necessary characteristic of the generous critic. As an aspect of generosity, it permits the critic to achieve a close emotional and intellectual kinship with the author under study: "No longer his

Interpreter, but *He*." The generous critic reads with a sympathetic understanding, which, when perfectly attuned, allows a presumptive reconstruction of authorial plans and purposes and processes which complement a judicious study of the text.[5]

In Pope's own words: "A perfect Judge will *read* each Work of Wit / With the same Spirit that its Author *writ*" (ll. 233-34). Even if the idea is parodied in *A Tale of a Tub*,[6] all authors devoutly wish for such sympathetic involvement on the part of their readers.

This "civilized" position may be as attractive to readers as to authors. The call for generosity and sympathetic understanding suggests humanity as it entails a subordination of the individual (or to use Pope's term, the part) to the whole, a giving of the self to something outside and larger. Certainly it is consonant with Pope's thematic focus, not only in *An Essay on Criticism* but also in *An Essay on Man* and the later *Dunciad*, as well as with his insistence on the moral qualities of the poet, all of which links him to that humanism that Aubrey Williams and others have ably described. As Morris argues, the task that Pope holds out for readers is the difficult one of subordinating oneself to and melding with the "Spirit" of the author. This "generous" position perhaps calls to mind what I wrote in the opening chapter concerning the need to attend to authorial declarations, first of all reading *with* the grain. But if the parallel initially appears close between the two positions, it soon ends, since I go on to propose what is evidently contrary to Pope's theory. Indeed, the opposite of such generosity of spirit as Pope advocates would seem to be not only the partiality, prejudice, and pride that he explicitly condemns but also the (apparently) correlative effort I manifest, whereby, after first attending to authorial declarations, we proceed to read *against* the grain. If the strategy I labeled, immodestly enough, reader-responsibility criticism first reads "With the same Spirit that [the] Author *writ*," it later sets out deliberately to violate that spirit. Ungenerously perhaps, it turns against the "Spirit" with which the author wrote, reading contrary to it, in fact.

If we read deconstructively, proceeding as I have urged, are we not then implicated in and convicted of the pride that Pope attacks? An answer to that question may not be so easy as supposed by those polemicists who regard "speculative" or "creative" criticism, and deconstruction in particular, as proud and overbearing, if not actually Satanic. This is not the place to debate the issue, but in passing I direct attention to, among other contexts for understanding deconstructive strategies and desires, Richard A. Lanham's account of "the rhetorical ideal of life," defined as both dramatic and competitive.[7] Here I shall argue that if we limit our reading of *An Essay on Criticism* to Pope's own declared "Spirit" and the principles he supports, we will not only miss much but also end with at best a *partial*—and impoverished—sense of the considerable achievement that is the *Essay.* At the same time, I insist that Pope has much to teach all readers about reading, including deconstructionists and traditional scholars. Reading "With the same Spirit that [the] Author *writ*" remains essential (at least as a first "step").

The Style Is the Man

I begin with what we might call, borrowing terms from Pope, the poem's "*Gen'rous Converse*" (l. 641). This phrase, which the Twickenham Edition glosses as "well-bred intercourse," occurs toward the end of *An Essay on Criticism* as Pope describes the "ideal critic," one who, while avoiding the pride and partiality the poet has lashed, bodies forth those qualities he has praised throughout. "Unbiass'd" and "Blest with a *Taste* . . . unconfin'd," the "ideal critic" enjoys "A *Knowledge* both of *Books* and *Humankind*" (ll. 633, 639-40). A whole person himself, in other words, such a critic effects an intercourse between qualities not always found combined in one man: he is "Still *pleas'd* to *teach*, and yet not *proud* to *know*," and "Tho' Learn'd, well-bred; and tho' well-bred, sincere; / Modestly bold, and Humanly severe" (ll. 632, 635-36).

An Essay on Criticism works toward a similar wholeness, blurring some distinctions too easily assumed to be absolute and seeking "*Gen'rous Converse*" between the various dichotomies it develops, including wit/judgment, poetry/criticism, sense/sound, and thought/language. The exacting scholarship on the poem has, of course, long pointed to the *complementariness* Pope works hard to establish between the poles of such dichotomies. Characterized by an apparent flexibility and a preference for "the complications rather than the simplifications of artistic truth," Pope's poem may be said "to harmonize the extremes and variables of critical thinking," aiming toward a "critical synthesis" and "the reconciliation of conflicting critical moods."[8] Complementariness, as well as generosity, appears when Pope declares, for instance, that "The *Sound* must seem an *Eccho* to the *Sense*" (l. 365) and that "The gen'rous Critick *fann'd* the *Poet's Fire*" (l. 100). Similarly, to take one more example, Pope writes that, even if "often . . . at strife," wit and judgment are "meant each other's Aid, like *Man* and *Wife*" (ll. 82-83).

Pope's entire effort in the *Essay* may stem from a perceived threat to such "*Gen'rous Converse*." That is, Pope addresses situations, mainly critical ones, of course, where complementariness has deteriorated into opposition. Thus he charges, for example, that if in a better past "The gen'rous Critick *fann'd* the *Poet's Fire*, / And taught the World, *with Reason* to *Admire*," the present is different, indeed "fallen":

> Then Criticism the Muse's Handmaid prov'd,
> To dress her Charms, and make her more belov'd;
> But following Wits from that Intention stray'd;
> Who cou'd not win the Mistress, woo'd the Maid;
> Against the Poets *their own Arms* they turn'd,
> Sure to hate most the Men from whom they *learn'd*.
>
> [ll. 102-7]

Against such antagonism Pope directs his efforts in the *Essay*, not only arguing, as we have already glimpsed, that wit and judgment are bound together, but also demonstrating that fact *in* writing criticism *as* poetry.

Noticing such attempts to effect complementary relations between dichotomous pairs, we approach an intellectual controversy that serves as a crucial backdrop against which *An Essay on Criticism* should be read. As is apparent in Pope's criticism of various tendencies to separate wit and judgment, language and thought, he challenges the attempts, in the work of philosophers and of members of the Royal Society alike, to drive a wedge between *res et verba*. As Aubrey Williams has written, "Slighting the theory that sense *informs* words, like the soul the body, the [seventeenth] century moves from Bacon's view that 'words are but the images of matter' to the Royal Society's repudiation of words in favour of things. From being the means to wisdom, words become obstacles to knowledge."[9] The tendency to divorce words from things, leaving language only a secondary and decorative function, received powerful support from Peter Ramus's influential re-definition of rhetoric. Ramus diverted invention and disposition from rhetoric to logic, which left the former only the diminished duty of "gilding the matter, the function of mere 'style' and delivery."[10] In philosophers like Hobbes and Locke, the powerful drive to sunder words and things takes the form of a debate over the respective capacities of wit and judgment, though the result is the same: an implicit "trivialization of poetry itself."[11] In such philosophers, according to Williams, "the faculty of Wit and the figurative language it inspires are seen as unrelated to truth and real knowledge, to 'things as they are.' Since figurative language is of the essence of poetry, the denial of its ability to express truth is the denial of the value and dignity of poetry. At best, the main role of Wit or of poetry becomes (as in Ramistic theory) the mere ornamentation of those truths provided for it by the judgment."[12] Since the humanist considered "the 'word' as 'wisdom' expressed," it was most important that any effort be confronted that would "empty eloquence of its wisdom, squeeze out of the word the thought it was believed to embody."[13] The way in which the humanist-rhetorical tradition regarded the word-thought relationship appears with particular clarity in the mid-century *British Education*, written by Thomas Sheridan, Swift's godson and father of the famous playwright. Stressing the "intimate connection between ideas and words," Sheridan claims that "the union of the soul and body are [*sic*] not more necessary for any useful purpose in life, than the union of oratory and philosophy for their mutual welfare." Somewhat more specifically, he writes, echoing Pope's particular concerns in *An Essay on Criticism*, that there is "such an intimate connection between ideas and words, language and knowledge, that whatever deficiency, or fault, there may be in the one, necessarily affects the other. . . . [May not the] corruption of our understandings [be owing] to those of our style? Are not our minds chiefly stored with ideas by words, and must not clearness or obscurity in the one, necessarily produce the same in the other?"[14]

In *Dunciad* IV, Pope presents as an accomplished fact the "decline of rhetoric into mere verbalism,"[15] critic, schoolmaster, and Dulness herself joining together in proudly proclaiming that "on Words is still our whole debate" (l. 219) and that they thus wage "war with Words alone" (l. 178). In *An Essay on Criticism* it is, less dramatically, a real and present danger. Directly addressing the perceived threat to wit, poetry, and figurative language, Pope pointedly defines "*True Wit*" as

> . . . *Nature* to Advantage drest,
> What oft was *Thought*, but ne'er so well *Exprest*,
> *Something*, whose Truth convinc'd at Sight we find,
> That gives us back the Image of our Mind.
> [ll. 297-300]

He is unsparing in lashing those who "unskill'd to trace / The *naked Nature* and the *living Grace*, / With *Gold* and *Jewels* cover ev'ry Part, / And hide with *Ornaments* their *Want of Art*" (ll. 293-96). Similarly, Pope rebukes those who "for *Language* all their Care express, / And value *Books*, as Women *Men*, for *Dress*" (ll. 305-6). Frequently employing the familiar metaphor of dress, which in fact becomes in the *Essay* the metaphor of metaphor, Pope follows a long and distinguished line of critics who so depict expression, Dryden, for one, writing that "expression . . . is a modest clothing of our thoughts, as breeches and petticoats are of our bodies."[16] In the *Essay*, Pope defines "true *Expression*" as that which, "like th' unchanging *Sun*, / *Clears*, and *improves* whate'er it shines upon, / It *gilds* all Objects, but it *alters* none. / Expression is the *Dress* of *Thought*" (ll. 315-18).

Reading such declarations in the context of the humanist-rhetorical tradition and the various contemporary assaults upon it, Aubrey Williams finds only complementariness. For Pope, he maintains, words *embody* thought. On this argument, the same notion informs bodies, Nature itself, and "expression"; that is, just as Nature figures forth God, so,

> In some fair Body thus th' informing Soul
> With Spirits feeds, with Vigour fills the whole,
> Each Motion guides, and ev'ry Nerve sustains;
> *It self unseen*, but in th' *Effects*, remains.   [ll. 76-79]

Claiming that "the style is the man," Williams evidently means that style, or "expression," mirrors perfectly and reflects accurately what one is, just as words incarnate thought. By no means mere ornamentation (as Hobbes, Locke, and others had recently proposed), despite the inside/outside, contained/container dichotomies that the metaphor of dress implies, words and the expression they constitute are, in this rather "Christian" formulation, not detachable from thought, sense, and meaning, even if thought can somehow exist without, and precede, language.

The Skidding of Meaning

But is the relationship one of embodiment and incarnation, as has been supposed? It is certainly true that at least at times in *An Essay on Criticism* Pope insists on the inseparability of thought and language, as well as of inside and outside. In one important passage, however, occurs a description establishing not the embodiment of preexistent thought in language but their interimplication. I refer to those verses in which Pope parallels poetry and painting, detailing the catastrophic effect of time on both media.[17] As in one, so in the other, Pope declares; since we have only *"failing Language,"* "such as *Chaucer* is, shall *Dryden* be":

> So when the faithful *Pencil* has design'd
> Some *bright Idea* of the Master's Mind,
> Where a *new World* leaps out at his command,
> And ready Nature waits upon his Hand;
> When the ripe Colours *soften* and *unite*,
> And sweetly *melt* into just Shade and Light,
> When mellowing Years their full Perfection give,
> And each Bold Figure just begins to *Live;*
> The *treach'rous Colours* the fair Art betray,
> And all the bright Creation fades away!   [ll. 482-93]

Though time initially exerts a positive effect on the artistic media, in fact mellowing *"Colours"* to "full Perfection," they eventually "fade" and ultimately disappear. As the *"Colours"* do so, Pope admits, they "betray" and, indeed, un-create the art that they *make.* Such destruction is possible in written texts, "fair Art's" *"Colours"* being equally *"treach'rous"* in them, only if, of course, language and its figures do much more than enhance, dress, or gild thought. Rather than body forth a preexistent thought, *"Colours"* are inseparable from it because they *create* it.

But the interimplication described in this passage does not principally characterize the relationship that obtains between language and thought in the *Essay.* If it is not one of interimplication, it is not unproblematically of inseparable links, either. Consider carefully the frequent dress metaphor that we have already noted. This particular metaphor clearly suggests a dichotomy and, indeed, an opposition of words and thought, with the latter existing as the inside, the former the outside. This opposition appears in Pope's remark in 1726 in a letter to Broome that "the most poetical dress whatever, will avail little without a sober fund of sense and good thought."[18] Paralleling various comments in *An Essay on Criticism*, this statement points to a hierarchical opposition in which thought is not only depicted as distinct from language but also privileged as prior to its formulation and expression in language. As a "fund," thought comes first, lies at bottom, and serves as ground. Repeating this familiar position, Williams writes that in the understanding of the humanist-rhetorical tradition "speech *reproduced* thought in words" (my italics).[19] No matter the argument elsewhere concerning the inseparability of words and thought, this statement reveals not only the logo- and phonocentric privileging of speech but also the assumption that thought is distinct from, prior to, and possible apart from language.

Even if "'tis hard to say" (l. 1) what certain differences are and to make necessary discriminations, it is clear that Pope regards thought and expression as distinct, albeit related, entities. Consider, first, some lines I quoted earlier, perhaps Pope's clearest statement on the relationship of language and thought: "true *Expression*, like th' unchanging *Sun*, / *Clears*, and *improves* whate'er it shines upon, / It *gilds* all Objects, but it *alters* none."[20] To echo Paul de Man writing in quite a different context, these lines must be *read*, not simply paraphrased.[21] To begin with, note that, even if, in clearing, improving, and gilding the objects it shines upon, the sun does not "alter" those objects, it obviously changes their appearance and thus inevitably our perception of and reaction to them. With expression, in any case, the situation is different: to claim *either* that expression does not "alter" *or* that it does amounts to the same thing; it assumes that expression and thought or meaning are distinct and separable and that thought is prior to its "expression" in language.

Essentially the same position appears in the following couplet: "Launch not beyond your Depth," Pope advises, "but be discreet, / And mark *that Point* where Sense and Dulness *meet*" (ll. 50-51). When read "analytically," as de Man recommends, Pope's assumption emerges clearly: it is that such differences as those between sense and dulness are absolute and that, though at some point they meet, they remain distinct. If they *meet* at some *point*, it is only *because* they are absolute distinctions. Were they each other's *différance*, as Derrida has argued concerning all binary oppositions, they could not meet at a point. For Pope, clearly, the desire is to mark the place where meeting occurs, and his act of creating the opposition sets meaning in place and keeps it from what might truly permit *"Gen'rous Converse"* and fruitful (if not well-bred) intercourse.

There are, though, no clear, distinct, and absolute lines of demarcation between dulness and sense (which is not to say, of course, that they are indistinguishable). Meaning refuses to stay still and in place; instead, it skids, and so no "point" exists where sense or dulness is simply "itself" or where these differences meet as distinct entities, let alone oppositions. I am reminded of the blind/insightful Hack who comments in *A Tale of a Tub* upon "how near the frontiers of height and depth border upon each other," how "one who travels the east [eventually runs] into the west," and how "a straight line [is eventually] drawn by its own length into a circle."[22] It is not, then, that sense and dulness, like those other pairs of difference treated in *An Essay on Criticism*, are simply *linked*, for the idea of linking presupposes distinction and, ultimately, separation. Rather, they are always already interimplicated, bound together, and cross in a constant movement. That this is so, that meaning refuses to stay in place, becomes clear in the second verse of the couplet we are reading: "Mark," Pope advises, "*that Point.*" A mark is, by definition, "a visible impression or trace upon something," and "to mark" is, for example, not only to notice or to heed but also (therefore) to single out, to make distinct, to put a mark on, "to trace or form by or as by marks" (*Random House Dictionary*). If one *marks* a point, does that point exist prior to the act of marking? The point marked may be, in other words, constituted and brought into "being" by the mark. The mark is, of course, writing, and as mark, writing is *creative* in a manner and to an extent that Pope certainly does not declare. Pope's language establishes, however, that marking, that is, writing, is performative, as well as mimetic. Pope creates the *point* between sense and dulness.

Another couplet in the *Essay* makes even clearer the power of performance. I refer to lines 574-75, where Pope grants the performative nature of his own earlier claims that knowledge and "the *Seeds* of Judgment" are born with human being, though "by *false Learning* is *good Sense* defac'd" (ll. 20, 25): "Men must be *taught* as if you taught them *not;* / And Things *unknown* propos'd as Things *forgot.*" Rather than a faithful mirroring of reality, Pope's claims regarding inherent judgment and knowledge are *propositions:* one *proposes* that the unknown is what one knew but forgot. The inside thus loses its privileged status, for performance, supposedly an outside perhaps analogous to "dress," emerges as creative in the same way as language.

Playing the Part

The power of performance, as of language, appears in the textual description woven by *An Essay on Criticism.* Pope's declarations, however, constitute quite a different story.

They tell, often at least, not of a complementary relation-
ship, as has been claimed, but of a particular kind of un-
generous relationship between thought and language.
That relationship Derrida depicts as characteristic of our
familiar dichotomies. "In a classical philosophical oppo-
sition," he writes, "we are not dealing with the peaceful
coexistence of a *vis-à-vis*, but rather with a violent hier-
archy. One of the two terms governs the other (axiologi-
cally, logically, etc.), or has the upper hand." Crucial to
dichotomies, according to Derrida, is "the conflictual and
subordinating structure of opposition." [23]

The dichotomies that structure *An Essay on Criticism*
participate fully in the situation that Derrida describes.
Not only thought/language but also sense/sound, wit/
judgment, poetry/criticism, and (hardly surprising) whole/
part reflect this characteristic hierarchical and opposi-
tional structure. Thus, if in "proper" poetry, "The *Sound*
must seem an *Eccho* to the *Sense*," the latter is privileged,
given priority (both metaphorically and literally), and
made dominant over sound, whose function is simply to
repeat. The relationship Pope stresses between parts and
whole captures that operative in the other dichotomies.
That is, as he does later in both *An Essay on Man* and
Dunciad IV, where the issue also figures prominently, Pope
reverses the hierarchizing that installs a favorite part in the
privileged position: "Most Criticks," he writes in *An Essay
on Criticism*, "fond of some subservient Art, / Still make
the *Whole* depend upon a *Part*" (ll. 263-64). What mat-
ters, Pope insists, "Is not th' Exactness of peculiar Parts; /
'Tis not a *Lip*, or *Eye*, we Beauty call, / But the joint Force
and full *Result* of *all*" (ll. 244-46). The part must, then,
sacrifice itself and submit to the whole.

Even if at first it appears generous and complementary,
the relationship of wit and judgment is characterized by
the same hierarchical structure. Though Pope claims that

they are "meant each other's Aid, like *Man* and *Wife*," he precedes this complementary account with the somewhat less generous statement that wit contains within itself the judgmental faculty or ability: "Some, to whom Heav'n in Wit has been profuse, / Want as much more, to turn it to its use" (ll. 80-81). That judgment is thus subordinated to wit is perhaps even clearer in the version of these lines that appeared in the poem from 1711 to 1743: "There are whom Heav'n has blest with store of Wit, / Yet want as much again to manage it." Unlike Hobbes and Locke, as well as certain of Pope's enemies who decried the alleged confusion in these lines, he obviously refuses to divorce wit and judgment. But the relationship between them is not so generous as is sometimes supposed.

Nor is that between poetry and criticism. As we have seen, Pope declares the complementariness between them: in ancient Greece, at least, "The gen'rous Critick *fann'd* the *Poet's Fire*." But if "Criticism the Muse's Hand-maid prov'd, / To dress her Charms, and make her more belov'd," its function was nevertheless subordinate, sub-servient, and so parallel to that involving expression and thought. The dress metaphor establishes criticism as, like language and expression, an outside whose task is to en-hance an inside. Criticism thus seems marginal.

Pope himself is, of course, writing criticism, but he does so—the obvious perhaps bears repeating—in poetic form, which indicates the privilege he affords poetry. Just as wit includes judgment, so poetry thus *encompasses* criticism. Indeed, from the beginning of the *Essay*, Pope contends that only those skilled in writing (poetry) should evaluate writing or teach others how to write: "Let such teach oth-ers who themselves excell," Pope declares, "And *censure freely* who have *written well*" (ll. 15-16). Writing well is, then, for Pope a necessary license for a critic. In this re-gard, the ideal is Horace:

He, who Supream in Judgment, as in Wit,
Might boldly censure, as he boldly writ,
Yet *judg'd* with *Coolness* tho' he sung with *Fire;*
His *Precepts* teach but what his *Works* inspire.

[ll. 657-60]

Moreover, in writing criticism, Pope brings together wit
and judgment, exhibiting wit in performing the critical
function and demonstrating—indeed, embodying—the
proper way to make critical judgments. As a matter of fact,
Pope draws in the attributes of the "ideal critic," amassing
to himself the qualities he praises. If any doubts remain
that the "speaking voice" of *An Essay on Criticism* embod-
ies those features Pope singles out as crucial in a critic,
they are surely dispelled as he ends the poem with an ex-
plicit account of himself. Acknowledging the support of
his friend Walsh, Pope recalls the earlier portrait of the
"ideal critic":

The Muse, whose early Voice you taught to Sing,
Prescrib'd her Heights, and prun'd her tender Wing,
(Her Guide now lost) no more attempts to *rise*,
But in low Numbers short Excursions tries:
Content, if hence th' Unlearn'd their Wants may view,
The Learn'd reflect on what before they knew:
Careless of *Censure*, nor too fond of *Fame*,
Still pleas'd to *praise*, yet not afraid to *blame*,
Averse alike to *Flatter*, or *Offend*,
Not *free* from Faults, nor yet too vain to *mend*.

[ll. 735-44]

Made clear in the poem's ethical appeal is Pope's intention
to achieve in and by means of it what he describes Lon-
ginus as accomplishing:

Thee, bold *Longinus*! all the Nine inspire,
And bless *their Critick* with a *Poet's Fire*.

An ardent *Judge,* who Zealous in his Trust,
With *Warmth* gives Sentence, yet is always *Just;*
Whose *own Example* strengthens all his Laws,
And *Is himself* that great *Sublime* he draws.

[ll. 675-80]

The ideal is, then, inside *An Essay on Criticism.* The
implications of this fact require careful consideration, es-
pecially as they bear on the parts/whole relationship. That
fact, in turn, is related to the way the poem imperialisti-
cally seeks closure and totality. The *Essay* not only tells us
how it is to be read (with the "Spirit" with which Pope
wrote, properly subordinating parts, however interesting
and compelling in themselves, to the whole), but it also
closes in upon itself, reflexively. What is involved as a re-
sult we need now to consider.

As it aggrandizes, privileges, and celebrates poetry, *An
Essay on Criticism* becomes what Cleanth Brooks has
called, referring to another poem, "an instance of the doc-
trine which it asserts." Like Donne's "The Canonization,"
which Brooks discusses, the *Essay,* in other words, "is both
[an] assertion and the realization of the assertion."[24] If
we read the poem, as Pope evidently intends, as a self-
reflexive embodiment of its own theoretical principles and
thematic assertions, we perform, according to Jonathan
Culler, the critical move "in which the text is shown to
describe its own signifying processes and thus said to
stand free as a self-contained, self-explanatory aesthetic
object that enacts what it asserts."[25]

For the New Criticism, of course, whose contribution to
Pope studies has been quite impressive, a poem's perform-
ance, dramatization, or embodiment of its own doctrines
and themes signals its wholeness, totality, and "organic
unity." Brooks's image for the free-standing, complete aes-
thetic object, which almost religiously fuses being and

doing, is, of course, the well-wrought urn. Against such a possibility, Derrida, de Man, and others have recently mounted compelling arguments denying that discourse can ever fully account for itself, or become present to itself, in an act of self-referentiality or self-possession. Performative and constative, doing and being, it has been claimed, cannot coincide. Either an excess or a lack always prevents closure.

Why this is so, and one reason (out of two or three we shall consider) why *An Essay on Criticism* does not achieve the closure and totality it seeks, becomes clear with the help of Culler's discussion of Brooks's essay on "The Canonization." Culler shows how, in Donne's poem, an excess prevents it from closing itself in. With "The Canonization"—the point applies equally to *An Essay on Criticism*—the excess occurs *in* the poem's becoming what it asserts and thematizes. The apparent unity and totality that Brooks labels a well-wrought urn exceeds "itself," for in celebrating itself as whole, the poem incorporates into what it is that very celebration. It may even be, as Culler claims, that "if the urn is taken to include the response to the urn, then the responses it anticipates . . . become a part of it and prevent it from closing."[26] At any rate, a self-reflexive text like *An Essay on Criticism* becomes other than—because more than—that whole it celebrates itself for being. Produced is self-difference: as Culler puts it, "The structure of self-reference works in effect to divide the poem [from] itself."[27]

Such self-reflexivity as characterizes Pope's *Essay* is produced by folds, by the poem's folding back upon itself, trying to fold itself up. When a text engages in such an effort, as Derrida has shown, "it creates . . . an 'invaginated pocket,' in which an outside becomes an inside and an inner moment is granted a position of exteriority."[28] Invagination Derrida defines as "the inward refolding of *la gaine* [sheath, girdle], the inverted reapplication of the outer edge to the inside of a form where the outside then opens a pocket."[29] The process of invagination is so complex that Derrida proceeds to "situate the place, the locus, in which *double invagination* comes about, the place where the invagination of the upper edge on its outer face . . . , which is folded back 'inside' to form a pocket and an inner edge, comes to extend beyond (or encroach on) the invagination of the lower edge, on its inner face . . . , which is folded back 'inside' to form a pocket and an outer edge."[30] Adopting Derrida's formulation, we might say that when *An Essay on Criticism* seeks to do and be what it describes and advocates, folding back upon itself, it creates an invaginated pocket. The outside thus becomes an inside, but if the outside comes inside, the inside is, then, not simply an inside. Nor is the outside merely an outside. As Derrida writes, putting the copula "under erasure," "The Outside I̶s̶ the Inside."[31] The implications should be clear as well for such oppositions as thought and expression, which enlist under the inside/outside figure. Since the parts of such dichotomies function not as opposed absolute distinctions but as each other's *différance*, a "trace" of the "one" always inhabiting the "other," there is no point at which completion or closure is or can be attained.

One need not, however, subscribe to Derrida's deconstructive insights (as compelling as they seem) to reach the same conclusion. From quite another angle, in fact, we can appreciate how *An Essay on Criticism* fails to achieve wholeness and closure. Recall, to begin with, that as David B. Morris and others have suggested, the *Essay* instructs the reader in how to read it. But if it does so, in one sense as writing it violates its own instruction in reading. Despite, that is, Pope's reiterated insistence that the reader "Survey the *Whole*," the poem fails to do what it asks the (its) reader to do: it does not subordinate all its parts to the whole. Indeed, the *Essay* as we have it could not have been written on Pope's declared principles, and if it is read only according to them, as Morris for one suggests, much is missed—so much that Pope himself obviously relishes. The point has to do with the purposiveness/play opposition that Pope sets up, and the best example of what amounts to a subversion (or deconstruction) of that opposition as well as of the whole/parts hierarchy occurs, ironically enough, in the poem's second section (lines 201-559). I say "ironically" because the whole/parts opposition is itself the center of discussion and in fact the organizing principle of the entire section, serving to link the seemingly disparate topics treated. Here the pyrotechnical display of wit and "expressiveness," offered by an ambitious young poet, calls attention to itself, with the effect that the reader inevitably looks *at* it, rather than *through* it to some putative whole to which it contributes and supposedly submits.[32] Interestingly, just before he discusses and demonstrates the "expressiveness" poetry can achieve, Pope criticizes those "Who haunt *Parnassus* but to please their Ear, / Not mend their Minds; as some to *Church* repair, / Not for the *Doctrine*, but the *Musick* there" (ll. 341-43). I quote the most strong-willed and unsubmissive lines:

> These *Equal Syllables* alone require,
> Tho' oft the Ear the *open Vowels* tire,
> While *Expletives* their feeble Aid *do* join,
> And ten low Words oft creep in one dull Line,
> While they ring round the same *unvary'd Chimes,*
> With sure *Returns* of still *expected Rhymes.*
> Where-e'er you find *the cooling Western Breeze,*
> In the next Line, it *whispers thro' the Trees;*
> If *Chrystal Streams with pleasing Murmurs creep,*
> The Reader's threaten'd (not in vain) with *Sleep.*
> Then, at the *last,* and *only* Couplet fraught
> With some *unmeaning* Thing they call a *Thought,*

> A *needless Alexandrine* ends the Song,
> That like a wounded Snake, drags its slow length
> along.
> Leave such to tune their own dull Rhimes, and know
> What's *roundly smooth*, or *languishingly slow;*
> And praise the *Easie Vigor* of a Line,
> Where *Denham's* Strength, and *Waller's* Sweetness join.
> True Ease in Writing comes from Art, not Chance,
> As those move easiest who have learn'd to dance.
> 'Tis not enough no Harshness gives Offence,
> The *Sound* must seem an *Eccho* to the *Sense.*
> *Soft* is the Strain when *Zephyr* gently blows,
> And the *smooth Stream* in *smoother Numbers* flows;
> But when loud Surges lash the sounding Shore,
> The *hoarse, rough Verse* shou'd like the *Torrent* roar.
> When *Ajax* strives, some Rock's vast Weight to throw,
> The Line too *labours*, and the Words move *slow;*
> Not so, when swift *Camilla* scours the Plain,
> Flies o'er th'unbending Corn, and skims along the
> Main.   [ll. 344-73]

These verses obviously problematize Pope's criticism of those who privilege language, conceits, numbers, and so forth, sacrificing a poetic whole to such parts. They in fact become *excessive,* Pope's own "part" here refusing, despite his repeated declarations, to subordinate itself to a reigning purposiveness. A purpose does, of course, exist for Pope's display of "expressiveness," but no such purpose can account for the extent of that effort. Like the Alexandrine Pope ridicules, at least much of what he writes in the quoted verses is "*needless.*" In them, at least, play triumphs over simple purposiveness. But I do not suggest that this play represents some failure of critical judgment, that Pope "wanted, or forgot, / The last and greatest Art, the Art to blot" (*Epistle to Augustus*, ll. 280-81). Far from it; failure to appreciate the excess the lines represent is an impoverishment of Pope's achievement, which transcends any simple sense of unity and wholeness. One final point: The view of language implicit in this "excessive" passage differs from that Pope declares in the poem. Whereas he generally privileges thought and sense over "expression" and sound, here, in looking at rather than through language, he approaches the Dunces' concentration on words as such.

Will Equivocation Undo Us?

Of course, as we have seen, Pope typically reverses the hierarchy being established by philosophers and scientists and privileges wit at the expense of judgment, poetry at the expense of criticism. Yet at the same time he elevates thought above language and "expression," which contradicts the "*at*" view of language implied in the long passage I just quoted. Indeed, the privileging of thought looks in a direction different from that implied in the privileging of wit and poetry; it looks away from poetry, in fact, and toward philosophy, the very position Pope is concerned in the *Essay* to confront and repudiate. Does Pope end up, then, doing what he indicts others for doing, threatening the very existence of poetry, in spite of himself?

The answer, confusingly enough, seems to be both yes and no. That is, an answer depends on whether you refer to the declaration or the (different) description. It would, I believe, be an oversimplification as well as a distortion to assume, therefore, that the equivocation or ambiguity results from Pope's immaturity, lack of control, or intellectual confusion, with all of which he has been (unfairly) charged and damned. The bottom line is that *An Essay on Criticism* equivocates; more, it oscillates, from one position to its supposed opposite. Even if such equivocation and oscillation are both more prominent and more blatant than in certain other texts, equivocation characterizes all texts, though the particular features and operation differ considerably. And even if Hamlet claims that "equivocation will undo us" (V.i.120-21), equivocation may be unavoidable.

Most important to grasp is the essential structure in all such oppositions as function in the *Essay* and Western thinking generally: the opposed pairs are not separable and distinct but interimplicated. Lest some misunderstanding remain, I repeat what the best scholarship on *An Essay on Criticism* has long maintained: at the "level" of declaration, Pope refuses to divorce wit and judgment, poetry and criticism, thought and expression. At the same time, however, the relationship between the "poles" in each dichotomy is not altogether complementary or simply generous. In each instance, in fact, a hierarchy appears, Pope normally reversing the privilege that at the time was being increasingly accorded to judgment and straightforward, referential language. With the dichotomy thought/language, however, Pope seems, in spite of his declarations to the contrary, on the side of his philosophical and scientific opponents. The latter position becomes clear through the kind of close reading that takes us beyond or behind Pope's declarations to the "counter" story being told by the textual description and that leads us not simply to a confirmation of Pope's declarations (i.e., oppositional terms are not separable) but to a position different from the declared one: namely, that the oppositional terms are not distinct but, rather, related as each other's *différance*. It is not, then, that wit and judgment *can* be combined and should be in order to prevent certain disastrous consequences. Rather, they always already *are* related, bound together, a "trace" of the "one" inevitably appearing in and inhabiting the "other."

❧ *Chapter Three*

"Some Strange Comfort"

Construction and Deconstruction
in An Essay on Man

Many of the concerns that structure *An Essay on Criticism* continue in *An Essay on Man*. Whereas the earlier poem reveals Pope's commitment to certain distinctions and oppositions, his theodicy revolves around his commitment to the notion of the "proper." This complex idea is itself related to Pope's central argument in *An Essay on Man* concerning God's impartiality, which runs counter to the human desire for and expectation of preferential—and differentiating—treatment. The work of difference in this later poem, in both Pope's declarations and the textual description, is more complicated, in part because, in *An Essay on Man*, deconstruction appears *in* those declarations, as an important theme.

The Vanity of Human Wishes

In "The Design" of *An Essay on Man*, Pope writes:

There are not *many certain truths* in this world. It is therefore in the Anatomy of the Mind as in that of the Body; more good will accrue to mankind by attending to the large, open, and perceptible parts, than by studying too much such finer nerves and vessels, the conformations and uses of which will for ever escape our observation. The *disputes* are all upon these last, and, I will venture to say, they have less sharpened the *wits* than the *hearts* of men against each other, and have diminished the practice, more than advanced the theory, of Morality. If I could flatter myself that this Essay has any merit, it is in steering betwixt the extremes of doctrines seemingly opposite.

Pope's account here of his approach to religious, philosophical, and ethical questions may be read as an allegory of the way the reading of his own poem should proceed, or at least the first "phase" in which we attend to "the large, open, and perceptible parts," at the expense of "such finer nerves and vessels" as constitute the narrow institutional and doctrinal questions that I formerly wished to study. Respecting Pope's desire to avoid the contentions and disputes arising from consideration of various "finer" differences, I begin with large issues, perhaps the largest ones possible. These include the question of how an ordinary mortal looks at and conceives of his or her world, his place in it, and his relation to everything around him: in short, how he feels about and in (to use Pope's term) a "universe" that is certainly daunting and a-mazing.[1]

For assistance in this complex undertaking, I draw on Herbert N. Schneidau's *Sacred Discontent: The Bible and Western Tradition.* With the insights of several disciplines, including critical theory, Schneidau explores the pervasive implications of differences between Hebraic and Biblical thinking, on the one hand, and, on the other, classical and pagan. The latter, he argues, possesses a mythological

consciousness, which characteristically "affirms conti-
nuity throughout all realms of existence." Positing a "con-
tinuum," "a cosmic ecology of universal interdepen-
dence," the mythological consciousness assures us that
"nothing is really fortuitous or meaningless, at bottom."[2]
Entailed is a cybernetic view of a closed world, into which
nothing new or threatening—like the kerygma—can
break.

"To discover myth," writes Schneidau, "is to apprehend
a sense of hidden significance and continuity, to feel that
one is stumbling on a treasury of lost and fascinating sym-
bols, or even to discover that the whole world is a system
of correspondences: in short, myth tantalizes us with the
suggestion that the world is a language which, when illu-
mined, we can learn to read."[3] With its linked analogies
and correspondences, mythological thinking "exhibits
strong metaphorical tendencies. The enmeshing and in-
terlocking of structures is coherently expressed in poetic
evocation of transferable, substitutable qualities and
names. In this world, movement tends to round itself into
totalization, impelled by the principle of closure."[4]

The Bible, Schneidau claims, is radically different. To
put the matter in terms that (at least superficially) recall
both Pope's point in *An Essay on Man* that we look "thro'
Nature, up to Nature's God" (3.432) and his satire in *The
Dunciad* directed against those who are not "to Nature's
Cause thro' Nature led" (4.468), the Bible insists that
signs "point beyond the natural order, even where that or-
der includes what we would call the miraculous. We are
not being invited to contemplate the powers of nature, as
we are by mythology: another realm of existence alto-
gether is what is suggested. Yahweh is not incarnated in
the appearances, nor do they function as symbolic keys to
him: they are neither continuous with him in any sense,

nor analogous to his essence. The 'cosmic continuum' is deliberately broken, the forms are arbitrary signals, and the arbitrariness is the point."[5]

The point may also be Saussure's, who showed that the relation between word and thing, signifier and signified, despite our expectation, is merely arbitrary.[6] In any case, in opposition to the comforting, closed mythological world view found all around them, the ancient Hebrews privileged openness, contingency, and the arbitrary. Their thinking, accordingly, inclines toward the metonymical; as Schneidau writes, aphoristically, "Where myth is hypotactic metaphors, the Bible is paratactic metonymies."[7] Among other things, for the Hebrews an unbridgeable gap exists between the world of the gods and human culture. No institution, even their own, no matter if divinely ordained, is sacred and exempt from questioning (is there a parallel here to Reb Derissa's claim that there is nothing outside textuality?).[8]

In place, then, of the "cultural glue" of the mythological consciousness, writes Schneidau, "what the Bible offers culture is neither an ecclesiastical structure nor a moral code, but an unceasing critique of itself. For this critique a certain cost must be paid: we habitually call this cost 'objectivity,' but its original name was alienation. This critique . . . evolved from deliberately chosen and painfully intense experience of alienation: as the prophet's sense of Yahweh weighs him down, he sees man as dust, man's strivings as futility, and he feels chosen, set apart, estranged."[9]

Unsettling, like the Hebrews themselves, who were always wandering, never settled, this vision is not likely to comfort or reassure. To use terms by now familiar: Yahwism, Hebraism, and a certain Christianity are a matter of absence, rather than presence, both the Ark and the Tomb always already being empty. Moreover, the relentless "sacred discontent" of the Bible is not merely different from the mythological consciousness; it also deliberately confronts such thinking and actively pursues a process of disillusioning us concerning one myth after another. Though there has been much talk, particularly in this century, of the need to de-mythologize the Bible, the Bible, as Schneidau argues, actually de-mythologizes us, shattering the myriad myths, illusions, and other consolations that we generally believe sustain us. The Bible is a relentless, unceasing critique of all our vanities.

Against Partiality, or the Work of Disillusionment

Almost everything we know, or at least have been taught, about Pope would suggest that he belongs with those subscribing to the mythic notion of a "cosmic continuum." He does, after all, valorize the myth of the Great Chain of Being, an idea that Schneidau mentions.[10] Still, we should not—as I have already hinted—too quickly consign the poet to the category of those in need of de-mythologizing or deconstructing. Whatever our later disposition, we should first attend to Murray Krieger's recent (though largely undeveloped) suggestion that characteristic of the eighteenth century is "a widely accepted myth and, in the period's best minds, the deconstruct[ion] of that myth (often in spite of—or along with—some lingering allegiance to it)."[11] As an example of such deconstruction, Krieger cites *An Essay on Man*. This poem, he writes,

seeks to use the epistles after the first to modify that epistle, which seeks utterly to reduce our confusing reality to the clarity of a perfect, if unresponsive, art world ("All Nature is but Art, unknown to thee"). What follows casts back intimations about the vanity of that confident human projection of cosmos which fills the first epistle. In the earliest lines of the second epistle there is an abrupt shift to the fragile human perspective against which the confident projection of Epistle One can no longer stand so confidently. Indeed, in light of those magnificent lines, very little confidence in human knowledge can be left standing.[12]

But the first epistle may not be quite so clear or confident as Krieger thinks, nor what follows quite so shaky, at least not in the terms posited in this suggestive account. It is, I think, too simple a story to claim that the important differences in *An Essay on Man* lie between the first epistle and the other three.

The entire poem may be seen, in fact, like the acts of Yahweh in Schneidau's formulation, as "an agent of disillusionment,"[13] with clear de-mythological and even deconstructive elements. These elements appear in various ways and at various levels of significance. We might note, to begin with, the anticipation of deconstructive insights in such lines as "All feed on one vain Patron, and enjoy / Th'extensive blessing of his luxury" (3.61-62), which succinctly establish the interdependence and interimplication of host and parasite that J. Hillis Miller has discussed.[14] At one point, Pope even seems to anticipate the Derridean position that, though logocentric notions must be deconstructed, they cannot be avoided or eliminated: only put *sous rature*. Thus, in discussing the relation of virtue and vice, Pope maintains that the distinction is by no means an absolute difference, capable of being arrested or frozen as an opposition:

> Tho' each by turns the other's bound invade,
> As, in some well-wrought picture, light and shade,
> And oft so mix, the diff'rence is too nice
> Where ends the Virtue, or begins the Vice.
>
> [2.207-10]

In keeping with deconstruction, in fact, Pope proceeds to argue even so that virtue and vice do not merely collapse into one another, becoming indistinguishable. They remain different though not absolutely distinct, being (in my terms) each other's *différance:*

> Fools! who from hence into the notion fall,
> That Vice or Virtue there is none at all.
> If white and black blend, soften, and unite
> A thousand ways, is there no black or white?
> Ask your own heart, and nothing is so plain;
> 'Tis to mistake them, costs the time and pain.
>
> [2.211-16]

Probably the poem's most important, and certainly its most sustained, work of disillusionment (and demythologizing) appears in the famous opening lines of Epistle II. Here Pope depicts man, the object (or subject) of mankind's "proper study" (l. 2) as, if not what Derrida calls *la brisure* (the hinge), certainly a both/and creature, one therefore that shares the basic nature of deconstruction:

> Plac'd on this isthmus of a middle state,
> A being darkly wise, and rudely great:
> With too much knowledge for the Sceptic side,
> With too much weakness for the Stoic's pride,
> He hangs between; in doubt to act, or rest,
> In doubt to deem himself a God, or Beast;
> In doubt his Mind or Body to prefer,
> Born but to die, and reas'ning but to err;
> Alike in ignorance, his reason such,
> Whether he thinks too little, or too much:
> Chaos of Thought and Passion, all confus'd;
> Still by himself abus'd, or disabus'd;
> Created half to rise, and half to fall;

> Great lord of all things, yet a prey to all;
> Sole judge of Truth, in endless Error hurl'd:
> The glory, jest, and riddle of the world!   [ll. 3-18]

Again like de Man and other deconstructionists, Pope recognizes that, though humankind must render judgments and make decisions, they will inevitably be erroneous. Error is simply as unavoidable as what precedes it, the need to decide.

Pope's de-mythologizing efforts in *An Essay on Man*, to which the passage just quoted contributes importantly, have not, I believe, been sufficiently appreciated in the commentary. It is clear, of course, that Pope attempts to put human beings "in their place," disabusing us of various grandiose illusions concerning our power and position. This he does by directly confronting anthropocentrism, claiming, as above, that we possess a both/and nature, rather than the single, univocal one we often proudly claim. Indeed, he writes, "Two Principles in human nature reign" (2.53). Just as we exist in tension (the ancient idea of *metaxy*, as Eric Voegelin reminds us),[15] between the angels above and the beasts below us, so we are composed of both self-love and reason, being passionate as well as reasonable creatures. Of the two, moreover, passion is the stronger (2.76), and, perhaps against rationalist pufferies then circulating, Pope declares, "What Reason weaves, by Passion is undone" (2.42). He goes on, in fact, to deny that anyone is preeminently virtuous (or completely vicious): "Virtuous and vicious ev'ry Man must be, / Few in th'extreme, but all in the degree" (2.231-32).

Further deflating us is the "ruling passion," "The Mind's disease," which is "cast and mingled with [our] very frame" (2.137-38). No matter how much we claim to follow reason, we are ruled by "one master Passion in the breast," which "Like Aaron's serpent, swallows up the rest" (2.131-32): before the ruling passion, we are essentially helpless. With it our vaunted autonomy is nothing more, nor less, than a fiction.

> Nature its mother, Habit is its nurse;
> Wit, Spirit, Faculties, but make it worse;
> Reason itself but gives it edge and pow'r;
> As Heav'n's blest beam turns vinegar more sowr;
> We, wretched subjects tho' to lawful sway,
> In this weak queen, some fav'rite still obey.
> Ah! if she lend not arms, as well as rules,
> What can she more than tell us we are fools?
> Teach us to mourn our Nature, not to mend,
> A sharp accuser, but a helpless friend!
> Or from a judge turn pleader, to persuade
> The choice we make, or justify it made;
> Proud of an easy conquest all along,
> She but removes weak passions for the strong.
>
> [2.145-58]

The implications of the ruling passion are no less devastating to our proud claims that virtuous actions proceed from a single, conscious choice: "Nature gives us (let it check our pride) / The virtue nearest to our vice ally'd" (2.195-96). We are, simply put, thoroughly mixed—and not so grand—creatures, lacking the autonomy of all-determining reason and having "light and darkness in our chaos join'd" (2.203). And "What shall divide" this chaos? Pope asks. The answer is not supportive of anthropocentric claims: "The God within the mind" (2.204). As Epistle I insists, employing the theatrical metaphor so important to the whole poem,[16] God directs the play that is human existence, having given us a script and assigned us a role. Our task is to play the assigned part. What ultimately matters, to both us and the whole, is how well we act our part.

Somewhat as in *An Essay on Criticism*, Pope plays again on the idea of "part," "parts," partiality, and impartiality. In doing so, he continues his de-mythologizing efforts. As Milton does in his own theodicy, Pope declares that the purpose of his poem is to "vindicate the ways of God to Man" (1.16; less juridical, perhaps, Milton wrote "justify"). Pope's vindication entails developing the point, *contra* God's detractors, that "Man's [not] imperfect, Heav'n in fault; / Say rather, Man's as perfect as he ought" (1.69-70). The point involves, in turn, the claim that no one rank, part, or link in the Great Chain of Being occupies a favored position; none is better than any other. Using a notion crucial to *An Essay on Criticism*, Pope iterates and reiterates that God is impartial. Indeed, he suggests, impartiality is the defining characteristic of Order: "HEAV'N's great view is One, and that the Whole" (2.238).

God thus sees "with equal eye, as God of all" (1.87), and in fact "connects, and equals all" (1.280). Man, however, wants—and expects—partiality and preferential treatment both for his species and for himself as an individual—in other words, he wants God to treat him differently from the way He treats other creatures and other individuals. Man is even willing, so strong is his partiality and individualism, to practice "Th' enormous faith of many made for one; / That proud exception to all Nature's laws, / T'invert the world, and counter-work its Cause" (3.242-44). In the face of such expected favoritism, Pope asks, "can a part contain the whole?" (1.32).

Pope seems to have written *An Essay on Man* as a response, not only to those who slight God, but also (and perhaps more directly) to those who in a sense expect too much of Him. Since much of the following discussion bears on the point, I shall here simply cite some of the ways, from throughout the poem, in which Pope directly confronts those who expect God to be partial to them, to treat them differently. For example, in lines that may reflect the influence of his Deist friend Bolingbroke, Pope turns the anthropocentric hope for special blessing into the special blessing of hope:

> Hope humbly then; with trembling pinions soar;
> Wait the great teacher Death, and God adore!
> What future bliss, he gives not thee to know,
> But gives that Hope to be thy blessing now.
> Hope springs eternal in the human breast:
> Man never Is, but always To be blest.   [1.91-96]

Such lines as these problematize the charge of easy optimism frequently levelled at the poem, including, of course, by Voltaire in *Candide*.

Elsewhere Pope is more pointed in answering those who expect God to single out man from among all His creatures for special favors and so to treat him differently. Contrary to what man all too often believes, other creatures were not made for him:

> Has God, thou fool! work'd solely for thy good,
> Thy joy, thy pastime, thy attire, thy food?
> Who for thy table feeds the wanton fawn,
> For him as kindly spread the flow'ry lawn.
> Is it for thee the lark ascends and sings?
> Joy tunes his voice, joy elevates his wings:
> Is it for thee the linnet pours his throat?
> Loves of his own and raptures swell the note:
> The bounding steed you pompously bestride,
> Shares with his lord the pleasure and the pride:
> Is thine alone the seed that strews the plain?
> The birds of heav'n shall vindicate their grain:
> Thine the full harvest of the golden year?
> Part pays, and justly, the deserving steer:
> The hog, that plows not nor obeys thy call,
> Lives on the labours of this lord of all.   [3.27-42]

Pope's-response to anthropocentric desires and expectations climaxes in the final epistle. Here he confronts the Providentialist view, at the time receiving wide circulation,[17] that God intervenes in the "particular" situations of individual men and women by, for example, preserving them from various natural disasters:

> Shall burning Ætna, if a sage requires,
> Forget to thunder, and recall her fires?
> On air or sea new motions be imprest,
> Oh blameless Bethel! to relieve thy breast?
> When the loose mountain trembles from on high,
> Shall gravitation cease, if you go by?
> Or some old temple, nodding to its fall,
> For Chartres' head reserve the hanging wall?
>
> [ll. 123-30]

Such thinking as he answers here reflects, in Pope's view, nothing else than pride. God simply does not operate in the ways man wants and expects. Pope says that His ways are "equal to all" and impartial, and he makes clear that riches are no more a sign of God's favor than poverty is an indication of His disfavor. Apparently being in some senses in-different, He is not involved in our lives in the manner our vanity posits.

Yet, Pope asserts in a passage that may serve to summarize his point, precisely such vanity and pride characterize both our sermons and our prayers:

> Here then we rest: "The Universal Cause
> "Acts to one end, but acts by various laws."
> In all the madness of superfluous health,
> The trim of pride, the impudence of wealth,
> Let this great truth be present night and day;
> But most be present, if we preach or pray.   [3.1-6]

The last couplet here seems especially pointed as it indicates both the depth and the pervasiveness of our natural but ultimately selfish quest for special favors from God.

"Our Proper Bliss"

The design of *An Essay on Man* thus makes impartiality the basis of its vindication of God and His order. According to the succinct, and elliptical, argument presented in the first epistle, certain consequences follow logically from the premise that "ORDER is Heav'n's first law" (4.49). Pope writes:

> Of Systems possible, if 'tis confest
> That Wisdom infinite must form the best,
> Where all must full or not coherent be,
> And all that rises, rise in due degree;
> Then, in the scale of reas'ning life, 'tis plain
> There must be, somewhere, such a rank as Man;
> And all the question (wrangle e'er so long)
> Is only this, if God has plac'd him wrong?   [ll. 43-50]

According to this argument, the existent order by no means creates imperfection; on the contrary, "Our proper bliss depends on what we blame" (l. 282): that is, our happiness is actually dependent on God's impartiality in creating separate ranks and in providing our own (proper) place in the nature of things. Though we may lack (and would like) some of the attributes characteristic of other ranks, we are given what is proper for our particular station. Relatively, then, though not absolutely, we are perfect. It follows, obviously, that in this system based on clear and distinct difference all other ranks enjoy the same *relative* perfection. Such is the central argument of Epistle

I, the remaining epistles proceeding to detail the exact na-
ture of man, being faithful to "The proper study of Man-
kind" (2.2). "The Design" to the poem declares unequiv-
ocally that "to examine the perfection or imperfection of
any creature whatsoever, it is necessary first to know what
condition and *relation* it is placed in, and what is the
proper *end* and *purpose* of its *being*."

The "*condition* and *relation*" of man Pope explains in
the opening of Epistle II: he is "Plac'd on this isthmus of
a middle state" (l. 3), between the beasts and the angels,
his happiness hanging on his grateful acceptance of his
middle state and nature. "To reason right," Pope asserts in
a line often misunderstood because taken out of context,
"is to submit" to that nature and condition (1.164). In
other words, "The bliss of Man (could Pride that blessing
find) / Is not to act or think beyond mankind" (1.189-90).

Our "Pride . . . reas'ning Pride" is the source of "our
error" (1.123) in being dissatisfied with our relative per-
fection. It impels us to seek what no rank has, absolute
perfection.

> All quit their sphere, and rush into the skies.
> Pride still is aiming at the blest abodes,
> Men would be Angels, Angels would be Gods.
> Aspiring to be Gods, if Angels fell,
> Aspiring to be Angels, Men rebel.   [1.124-28]

When men do not find what they yearn for, they blame
God for their condition, necessitating such efforts as
Pope's to "vindicate the ways of God to Man" (1.16). Pope
finds the familiar human response ridiculous:

> Go, wiser thou! and in thy scale of sense
> Weigh thy Opinion against Providence;
> Call Imperfection what thou fancy'st such,
> Say, here he gives too little, there too much;

Destroy all creatures for thy sport or gust,
Yet cry, If Man's unhappy, God's unjust;
If Man alone ingross not Heav'n's high care,
Alone made perfect here, immortal there:
Snatch from his hand the balance and the rod,
Re-judge his justice, be the GOD of GOD!   [1.113-22]

"Is Heav'n unkind to Man, and Man alone?" Pope asks:
"Shall he alone, whom rational we call, / Be pleas'd with
nothing, if not bless'd with all?" (1.186-88).

Pope's argument involves the explicit claim that differ-
ence among the ranks of existent things, far from connot-
ing imperfection and leading to unhappiness, is actually
essential to each creature's "bliss." Pope makes clear the
implications of this point for man:

Heav'n to Mankind impartial we confess,
If all are equal in their Happiness:
But mutual wants this Happiness increase,
All Nature's diff'rence keeps all Nature's peace.
                                              [4.53-56]

Indeed, Pope claims the necessity of social, political,
and economic differentiation, echoing Ulysses' famous
speech, in *Troilus and Cressida,* on the role of distinctions
in human existence ("O when Degree is shaked / Which
is the ladder to all high designs, / The enterprise is
sick!").[18] Whether or not like Shakespeare, Pope would
evidently preserve class differences as essential to social
order: "Fortune's gifts if each alike possest, / And each
were equal, must not all contest?" (4.63-64).

Whatever we think of this particular position, it is
Pope's claim that we have our own place in the grand
scheme of things and that it is *proper* in that it is both our
own and appropriate to and for us: "God, in the nature of
each being, founds / Its proper bliss, and sets its proper

bounds" (3.109-10). As we have seen in circumstance
after circumstance, underlying Pope's argument is the be-
lief that what ultimately matters is not what an entity is or
how it is placed but rather what it does and how it acts in
its given situation. As he says in discussing the fact and
relation of reason and self-love, maintaining that the for-
mer merely restrains whereas the latter motivates and
urges:

> Nor this a good, nor that a bad we call,
> Each works its end, to move or govern all:
> And to their proper operation still,
> Ascribe all Good; to their improper, Ill.   [2.55-58]

Operating Properly

Man's "proper operation," the part he has been assigned
to play, entails the recognition that he is by no means an
island unto himself. Quietly transforming the Great
Chain of Being into "the chain of Love" (3.7), Pope asserts
that mutual dependency characterizes our "universe" (his
terms echo those used to describe Nature in *An Essay on
Criticism*):

> Nothing is foreign: Parts relate to whole;
> One all-extending, all-preserving Soul
> Connects each being, greatest with the least;
> Made Beast in aid of Man, and Man of Beast;
> All serv'd, all serving! nothing stands alone;
> The chain holds on, and where it ends, unknown.
>   [3.21-26]

As for man in particular, he is, Pope maintains, dependent
on others for the satisfaction of his needs, material and

otherwise, and ultimately for the "proper operation" of his own and his kind's being:

> Heav'n forming each on other to depend,
> A master, or a servant, or a friend,
> Bids each on other for assistance call,
> 'Till one Man's weakness grows the strength of all.
> Wants, frailties, passions, closer still ally
> The common int'rest, or endear the tie:
> To these we owe true friendship, love sincere,
> Each home-felt joy that life inherits here.   [2.249-56]

In such dependency resides man's opportunity for the happiness that is his "being's end and aim" (4.1). To achieve it, he must accept the opportunity and act on it. God built it into the very nature of things, having "fram'd a Whole, the Whole to bless, / On mutual Wants built mutual Happiness" (3.111-12).

Pope's is no mean insight: the bliss that it is in man's nature to seek for himself derives from his acceptance of his fate as coming "into being with his entry into related-ness, which is his entry into humanity."[19] It all begins, paradoxically, from self-love, which "but serves the vir-tuous mind to wake" (4.363). If properly "operated," it will, like the expanding circles created by a pebble dropped into a lake, "rise from Individual to the Whole" (4.362), moving outward, Pope claims, from "Friend, par-ent, neighbour" (4.367) to

> His country next, and next all human race,
> Wide and more wide, th'o'erflowings of the mind
> Take ev'ry creature in, of ev'ry kind;
> Earth smiles around, with boundless bounty blest,
> And Heav'n beholds its image in his breast.
>   [4.368-72]

Thus, the self-love that is fundamental in man can "be the same" as "Social" (3.318), and man, in fact, finds "the private in the public good" (3.282). In transforming self-love into charity, man finds happiness, fulfilling the law of Order, which is "the chain of Love":

> Self-love thus push'd to social, to divine,
> Gives thee to make thy neighbour's blessing thine.
> Is this too little for the boundless heart?
> Extend it, let thy enemies have part:
> Grasp the whole worlds of Reason, Life, and Sense,
> In one close system of Benevolence:
> Happier as kinder, in whate'er degree,
> And height of Bliss but height of Charity.   [4.353-60]

A stunted self-love, one that has not expanded outward but instead has constricted into a destructive concern for the good of one (the part) manifests itself in the desire for preferential treatment that has occasioned Pope's theodicy. Mankind's task remains, however, clear, proper, and manageable; it is to mirror in our relations with each other God's relation with us.

> Remember, Man, "the Universal Cause
> "Acts not by partial, but by gen'ral laws;"
> And makes what Happiness we justly call
> Subsist not in the good of one, but all.
> There's not a blessing Individuals find,
> But some way leans and hearkens to the kind.
>   [4.35-40]

Appropriately Comforting

If human happiness is, contrary to our vain expectations, dependent on God's impartiality, "Fix'd to no spot is Happiness sincere, / 'Tis no where to be found, or ev'ry where" (4.15-16). Since "to all Men Happiness was meant, / God in Externals could not place Content" (4.65-66). Thus writes Pope, continuing the Aristotelianism prominent as well in *An Essay on Criticism*, "Condition, circumstance is not the thing; / Bliss is the same in subject or in king" (4.57-58). The entire fourth epistle of *An Essay on Man* becomes an extended argument that happiness is not tied to being in any particular condition, state, or location or to having any possession.

Because, so the argument goes, "ORDER is Heav'n's first law," "Some are, and must be, greater than the rest, / More rich, more wise" (ll. 49-51). But, Pope insists, "who infers from hence / That such are happier, shocks all common sense" (ll. 51-52). Though he allows an imagined interlocutor to raise an objection, Pope advances the idealist argument that "'Virtue alone is Happiness below'" (l. 310). Pope's response to the caveat links up with his primary arguments in the poem, rebuking again the insatiable human drive for more. In fact, Pope makes the objection to his own argument part of what becomes both a selfish and a ridiculous set of expectations centering on "Externals" at the expense of virtue, which is an "internal" matter. As part of his satirical technique here as well as elsewhere, Pope "allows" his imagined respondent to expose himself.

> "But sometimes Virtue starves, while Vice is fed."
> What then? Is the reward of Virtue bread?
> That, Vice may merit; 'tis the price of toil;
> The knave deserves it, when he tills the soil,
> The knave deserves it when he tempts the main,
> Where Folly fights for kings, or dives for gain.
> The good man may be weak, be indolent,
> Nor is his claim to plenty, but content.

> But grant him Riches, your demand is o'er?
> "No—shall the good want Health, the good want
>   Pow'r?"
> Add Health and Pow'r, and ev'ry earthly thing;
> "Why bounded Pow'r? why private? why no king?"
> Nay, why external for internal giv'n?   [ll. 149-61]

As he proceeds, Pope becomes more and more satirical, lashing those who foolishly imagine the reward of virtue to be one of several "Externals." He promotes the anti-materialist contention that possession of such "Externals" may actually be detrimental to virtue.

> What nothing earthly gives, or can destroy,
> The soul's calm sun-shine, and the heart-felt joy,
> Is Virtue's prize: A better would you fix?
> Then give Humility a coach and six,
> Justice a Conq'ror's sword, or Truth a gown,
> Or Public Spirit its great cure, a Crown.
> Weak, foolish man! will Heav'n reward us there
> With the same trash mad mortals wish for here?
> The Boy and Man an individual makes,
> Yet sigh'st thou now for apples and for cakes?
> Go, like the Indian, in another life
> Expect thy dog, thy bottle, and thy wife:
> As well as dream such trifles are assign'd,
> As toys and empires, for a god-like mind.
> Rewards, that either would to Virtue bring
> No joy, or be destructive of the thing:
> How oft by these at sixty are undone
> The virtues of a saint at twenty-one!   [ll. 167-84]

Pope goes on to detail each of several "Externals" in which happiness is mistakenly thought to consist. These include riches, honor ("Honour and shame from no Condition rise; / Act well your part, there all the honour lies," ll. 193-94), titles, "greatness," and fame. Yet, despite the mad pursuit of such "trash," virtue remains "The only point where human bliss stands still" (l. 311). Because, Pope repeats, God is impartial, happiness is equal and available to all: "the sole bliss Heav'n could on all bestow; / Which who but feels can taste, but thinks can know" (ll. 327-28).

As he argues that no single state or condition assures one of happiness, happiness being trans-situational, Pope contends that no one form of government or of religion is privileged. What matters here too is not the outward manifestation or appearance (or the dress, the term most often used in similar contexts in *An Essay on Criticism*) but the "proper operation," the internal working, of the form or mode. In lines that offered little comfort to (many of) his fellow Catholics, Pope declares:

> For Forms of Government let fools contest;
> Whate'er is best administer'd is best:
> For Modes of Faith, let graceless zealots fight;
> His can't be wrong whose life is in the right:
> In Faith and Hope the world will disagree,
> But all Mankind's concern is Charity:
> All must be false that thwart this One great End,
> And all of God, that bless Mankind or mend.
>
> [3.303-10]

As usual in Pope, the internal is privileged, the external marginalized.

Confusing Things

This perhaps deliberately deconstructive but certainly disillusioning attempt to expose the vanity and the futility of the human wish for preferential and differentiating treatment turns out to be a rather comforting poem—even if the verses just quoted disturbed at least some Catholics. *An Essay on Man* not only links happiness with the very impartiality that shatters man's expectation of special favors from God, but it also confidently tells us exactly how we may assure ourselves of true happiness. "Our proper bliss depends," Pope declares, "on what we blame" (1.282). In our limitations lies our perfection.

Even, then, as it exposes one human construction and vanity, *An Essay on Man* creates another. It substitutes, in other words, one consolation for another, perpetuating contentment (an ever-present danger) rather than instilling the "sacred discontent" characteristic of both the Bible and deconstruction. The end of Epistle II focuses on the way we humans supplement, always searching, sometimes desperately, for something to comfort, console, and sustain us—and always finding a substitute for what we lack. Such supplementarity, Pope makes clear, is as pervasive as it is insistent. Whether or not religion is the opium of the people, as Marx claimed, it becomes, at least with age, a favored comfort, Pope maintains. I must quote the entire concluding section of the epistle, which is devoted to this important point concerning supplementarity:

> See some strange comfort ev'ry state attend,
> And Pride bestow'd on all, a common friend;
> See some fit Passion ev'ry age supply,[20]
> Hope travels thro', nor quits us when we die.
>   Behold the child, by Nature's kindly law,
> Pleas'd with a rattle, tickled with a straw:
> Some livelier play-thing gives his youth delight,
> A little louder, but as empty quite:
> Scarfs, garters, gold, amuse his riper stage;
> And beads and pray'r-books are the toys of age:
> Pleas'd with this bauble still, as that before;
> 'Till tir'd he sleeps, and Life's poor play is o'er!
>   Mean-while Opinion gilds with varying rays

Those painted clouds that beautify our days;
Each want of happiness by Hope supply'd,
And each vacuity of sense by Pride:
These build as fast as knowledge can destroy;
In Folly's cup still laughs the bubble, joy;
One prospect lost, another still we gain;
And not a vanity is giv'n in vain;
Ev'n mean Self-love becomes, by force divine,
The scale to measure others wants by thine.
See! and confess, one comfort still must rise,
'Tis this, Tho' Man's a fool, yet GOD IS WISE.

[ll. 271-94]

This remarkable, and ironic, passage is a devastating de-construction of human constructions (including decon-struction itself whenever it forgets its being as questioning or criticism as such), which masquerade of course as fact and truth. Not the least important of the ironies here, of the deconstruction being performed, is that which cannot be reasonably attributed to Pope's conscious intentions. Though he *declares* the deconstructive point that human activity consists of constant supplementing, his text sys-tematically inscribes the *description* that his own (proper) argument is unacknowledgeably what he ridicules, an-other supplement, and "some strange comfort." He ad-mits, after all, that "one comfort still must rise, / 'Tis this, Tho' Man's a fool, yet GOD IS WISE." What Pope has of-fered, then, in arguing for God's impartiality, on which, he insists, human happiness depends, is no less a supple-ment (or supply, the term he twice uses in the passage quoted), a consolation, and a comfort than the "beads and pray'r-books" he mentions here and the illusions that he elsewhere deplores "if we preach or pray" (3.6).

The *constructed* nature of our most cherished truths, and indeed the performative nature on which *An Essay on Man*—like *An Essay on Criticism*—stands, however unsteadily, appears as well in that important passage (1.43-50) I quoted earlier, in which Pope works out rationally a justification for man's place in the scheme of things. These verses make clear the *suppositional* nature of Pope's entire argument, which hangs on a set of propositions beginning with the *hypothesis* that "a God of infinite wisdom exists" who "will necessarily have chosen to create, out of all possible systems, the best." These propositions continue, according to Maynard Mack, whom I have been quoting, with the further hypothesis that "the best will necessarily have been that which actualizes the maximum number of possible modes of being, and so is 'full' of existents—a *plenum formarum*—'cohering' because actualization of all the possibles leaves no gaps." The final proposition holds that "the *plenum*'s structure is hierarchical, a ladder of beings of greater and greater complexity of faculties, rising by even steps (*due degrees*) from nothingness . . . to God."[21] What seems so natural as we read is actually a story, a construction of man.

Even if such accounts as Pope's are fictions, we are, he declares unequivocally, dependent on them. But the very notion of dependency, on which so much of *An Essay on Man* depends, is itself highly problematical. The poem maintains, as we saw, that each existent being is dependent on others, "Heav'n forming each on other to depend." If this is so, if indeed "nothing stands alone," then nothing is either self-sufficient or complete. If it cannot stand alone, it has a gap that needs supplementing, and is, therefore, in need of help from outside itself. The internal requires the external. If it is, then, variously dependent, it is not completely itself, or proper. It has, in fact, no proper self. This is all suggested in the innocent-looking line I quoted earlier, in which Pope both says that and shows how the host feeds on the parasites feeding on him: "All feed on one vain Patron," the adjective establishing the interimplication that J. Hillis Miller has demonstrated in the host/parasite relationship.

We should recall, moreover, that Pope has depicted man's "in-between" or middle nature, his contingency, in terms of the same root notion that functions in "dependency." Man "hangs between," Pope writes, signifying that man is neither angel nor beast but rather a little of both. If he is both one thing and another, he lacks a *proper* being. If this is so, Pope's entire chain of reasoning, starting with a thing's "proper *end* and *purpose* of its *being*," begins to deconstruct.

As a matter of fact, the notion of the "proper," so important to Pope's theodicy, is revealed as improper. Like the idea of dependency, which assumes a relationship between distinct and separable entities, being quite a different concept from interimplication, the "proper" depends on the existence of clear lines that allow for absolute differences, no matter the strength of the desire to collapse them. Pope unequivocally establishes his position in the first epistle of *An Essay on Man* when he declares: "What thin partitions Sense from Thought divide: / And Middle natures, how they long to join, / Yet never pass th' insuperable line!" (ll. 226-28). The "insuperable line" always already exists, according to Pope, making the "proper" possible.

That line also makes possible God's touted impartiality, but *is* it clear, distinct, and "insuperable," differentiating impartiality absolutely from partiality—and Pope from those he opposes? As we saw, Pope vigorously challenges the anthropocentric desire for differentiating treatment from God, insisting that He acts impartially, respecting no difference or distinction between individuals, groups, or species. In attitude, impartiality certainly suggests indifference, but it is in fact built on the notion of the "proper," which in all its forms Derrida has deconstructed;[22] that is, impartiality presupposes the possibility of choosing, it assumes separateness, and it is impossible unless a thing can be only its (proper) self and not also something else. Pope's argument directed against anthropocentric desires and expectations is thus interimplicated with (and contaminated by) what it opposes. Both the desire for differentiating treatment and the opposed argument for impartiality derive from a belief in clear, unequivocal distinction and difference. If in arguing against partiality, Pope seemed to oppose difference, he in fact links up with it. That result is not, finally, surprising, for any *oppositional* structure ends in *différance*. In spite of himself, therefore, Pope resembles those he opposes. Both he and the reviled anthropocentrists share a commitment to difference, the major difference between them perhaps being that Pope's desire is subtler and operates at a deeper enabling level.

There are, then, as John Dominic Crossan has written, "not only different differences but also different understandings of difference itself."[23] *An Essay on Man* indicates the difference between *différance* and both indifference and impartiality, which, though bearing some resemblance to Derrida's deconstruction of difference, are logocentrically based in adherence to unequivocation. *Différance* "precedes" difference and indeed makes it possible, "appearing" *within* Pope's argument as the latter both opposes anthropocentric differentialism and shares its presuppositions. That which is differentiated is linked by the disjunction just as what is linked is differentiated by that linking.[24]

An Essay on Man may most resemble *An Essay on Criticism* in the way it differs from "itself."[25] In Schneidau's terms, it is alienated from "itself" and calls into question the notion of the "proper," of identity, of absolute difference. The *Moral Essays* pursue such questions, focusing

on the quest of truth, dependent—apparently—on dis-
tinct lines and clear differences, and both *An Epistle to Dr.
Arbuthnot* and the *New Dunciad* return to "th' insuperable
line" between self and other, focusing on the crossing that
An Essay on Man shows to occur between supposed op-
posites. Part of the truth sought may be, as *To a Lady* puts
it, that "one" *is* "whate'er she hates and ridicules" (l. 120).

& *Chapter Four*

Shooting at Flying Game

*Reading and the Quest of Truth
in the* Moral Essays

I begin, no doubt unpromisingly, with my title. Whether it refers, like the title of this book, to Pope's efforts in these poems, to my own attempt to read them, or to both is a question I will not (presume to) answer. My title here comes from the *Epistle to Cobham,* specifically from a passage concerned with the difficulty we experience in reaching decisions and making judgments. First Pope declares that "God and Nature only are the same"; then he proceeds to grant the difference from such unity and identity ("I am who I am") that is man, in whom, contrariwise, "the judgment shoots at flying game, / A bird of passage! gone as soon as found, / Now in the Moon perhaps, now under ground" (ll. 154-57). It is precisely this difficulty in deciding that I wish to focus on in considering the four poems known as the "Ethic Epistles" and, in the Twickenham Edition, from which I quote, as the *Epistles to Several Persons.* Because of both its specificity and its brevity I prefer and will use the term *Moral Essays.*

Especially in these poems, deciding is related to the quest of truth, and that quest appears here most often as an issue in reading. *Cobham*, in particular, declares that man is not only different from God and Nature but that that difference derives from his own difference within, from his self-difference. Such difference produces the difficulty encountered in the attempt to read him and to arrive at the truth concerning him, his actions, and his motives. The job of deciding, including about the *Moral Essays*, is hard work, indeed. That in reading these poems we must contend with both Pope's declarations and the textual descriptions, with both construction and deconstruction, the latter at more than one level, makes the job all the more difficult. As in *An Essay on Man*, so here too Pope sometimes assumes stances parallel to deconstruction.

And like *An Essay on Criticism* and *An Essay on Man*, the *Moral Essays* pose the question of the relationship of parts to parts and of parts to whole. They do so, though, not so much through explicit thematization as through the question they direct to their reader about his or her reading *of them*. That is, four different but linked poems constitute the *Moral Essays*, which are in turn clearly related, thematically and figurally, to *An Essay on Man*. All eight poems, the late Miriam Leranbaum cogently argued, may form an important part of an "*Opus Magnum*" that Pope planned but never finished.[1] On this reading, the *Moral Essays* are seen as posing questions of the relationship of the four "parts" comprising this particular "whole" to each other, of the relationship of the four of them—both individually and collectively—to the four epistles of *An Essay on Man*, and of the relationship, finally, of all eight poems to the Horatian *Imitations* and even *The Dunciad*.

In the Preface to this book, I expressed my reservations concerning any attempt to posit a totality or unified whole to which various poems somehow contribute. The effort to attend to *relationships* among individual and different poems is, as I have stated, quite another matter,[2] and in the pages that follow I shall attend to common concerns among the *Moral Essays*, as well as to themes and notions shared with previous and later poems, but I do not see these poems relating to any whole other than the corpus of texts we identify as Pope's. I shall first focus on the topic of reading as it appears throughout these poems. Then I shall attempt a full-scale reading of the *Epistle to Bathurst*, at least arguably the richest and most rewarding of the *Moral Essays*.

Stalking the Unwobbling Pivot

In whatever order they were composed and printed[3] and however they are to be related, the *Moral Essays* treat, according to the "Argument" Pope affixed to each poem, "*the* Knowledge *and* Characters *of* Men" (*Cobham*), "the Characters of *Women*" (*To a Lady*), and "*the* Use *of* Riches" (both *Bathurst* and *Burlington*). In these poems, Pope obviously continues the effort central to (if not begun in) *An Essay on Man* to try to make sense of man, his actions, and his "universe." As it is in so many texts, from *Oedipus* to *Hamlet* and on to *Great Expectations* and beyond, reading is both an explicit theme and a central metaphor for this important exploration.[4]

In "The Design" to *An Essay on Man* Pope remarks that his theodicy "is only to be considered as a *general Map* of MAN, marking out no more than the *greater parts*, their *extent*, their *limits*, and their *connection*." He has, he writes, left "the particular to be more fully delineated in the charts which are to follow." *An Essay on Man*, Pope continues, has merely "open[ed] the *fountains*, and

clear[ed] the passage." What follows—that is, the "ethic
epistles"—will aim "To deduce the *rivers*, to follow them
in their course, and to observe their effects." Through the
characters of such men and women, fictional or otherwise,
as Wharton, Martha Blount, John Kyrle, Balaam, and Ti-
mon, Pope traces the particular rivers, charting their
course, attempting to locate their source, and exploring
their impact. The map imagery Pope employs in this ac-
count may, in the confidence it projects, belie the difficulty
of the job of reading entailed. Each of the epistles is con-
structed around "portraits" of individuals whose charac-
ters are particularly difficult to read, their actions appear-
ing so various and even contradictory. Pope suggests the
difficulty involved when he writes, in the "Argument" of
To a Lady, that the characters of women "are yet more
inconsistent and incomprehensible than those of Men."

Now printed as the first of the *Moral Essays*, *An Epistle
to Cobham* introduces the difficult attempt to read human
beings, their actions, and their motivations. The poem is,
in fact, an extended discussion of the (surprising) incon-
sistencies and the apparent incomprehensibility of the
characters of men. As he begins to consider the problem,
Pope warns us not to forget the observer in the observa-
tion; that is, he points to the complications caused by var-
iability and partiality in the observer. Pope sounds a mod-
ern theme in granting that reading consists of much more
than an objective processing, or decoding, of a passive
text. The observer—or reader—of human beings and
their actions is himself or herself a human being, sharing
the passions, opinions, and whims of those he studies;
there is simply no way for the reader to get outside, to a
neutral, objective position:

> Men may be read, as well as Books too much.
> To Observations which ourselves we make,

> We grow more partial for th' observer's sake;
> To written Wisdom, as another's, less:
> Maxims are drawn from Notions, these from Guess.
>
> [ll. 10-14]

The reader's opinions and desires, Pope continues, inevitably color the text. Because reading involves both a text and a reader, and is a matter of interpretation rather than of identification and repetition, there is no "fit" between the reading and the text read:

> Yet more; the diff'rence is as great between
> The optics seeing, as the objects seen.
> All Manners take a tincture from our own,
> Or come discolour'd thro' our Passions shown.
> Or Fancy's beam enlarges, multiplies,
> Contracts, inverts, and gives ten thousand dyes.
>
> [ll. 23-28]

What occurs in the reader, destroying the possibility of objectivity and the simple presentation of "truth," also occurs in the text studied. It is, in a word, difference, and it constitutes the major problem in the determined drive to read the characters of men (and of women, for that matter). If Pope sounds modern in advising us to grasp the reader's implication in the reading, he appears deconstructive in declaring that, no matter how careful and sophisticated our observations and interpretations are, something will not quite fit, will stubbornly remain on the "outside," refusing to be drawn neatly into the "whole" we strive vainly to make. It may be a gap, a hole, or perhaps some excess that destroys any sense of putative harmony and totality.

> There's some Peculiar in each leaf and grain,
> Some unmark'd fibre, or some varying vein:

Shall only Man be taken in the gross?
Grant but as many sorts of Mind as Moss.   [ll. 15-18]

Lest any doubt remain that Pope means to indicate, not just the difference *among* men, but also the difference *within* each man, note the following verses, in which Pope anticipates Barbara Johnson's use, cited earlier, of this very notion in characterizing the work of deconstruction:

> That each from other differs, first confess;
> Next, that he varies from himself no less:
> Add Nature's, Custom's, Reason's, Passion's strife,
> And all Opinion's colours cast on life.   [ll. 19-22]

Thus Atossa is "Scarce once herself, by turns all Womankind!" (*To a Lady*, l. 116).

From this account of the general difficulties difference and self-difference pose for the quest of truth about men, Pope turns to certain specific, and more technical, problems in reading. These include the impossibility of imposing a pattern on the process and flux of life. Experience, Pope suggests, does not easily—if at all—lend itself to the human compulsion to order and comprehend:[5]

> Our depths who fathoms, or our shallows finds,
> Quick whirls, and shifting eddies, of our minds?
> Life's stream for Observation will not stay,
> It hurries all too fast to mark their way.
> In vain sedate reflections we would make,
> When half our knowledge we must snatch, not take.
>   [ll. 29-34]

We normally expect, Pope continues, that the key to the truth about a man's character lies in his action. If we can but locate and isolate his "Principle of action," we should be able to read him correctly. *An Essay on Criticism*, we recall, stressed that proper attention to the purposive movement of literary texts will reveal the "Spirit [with which the] Author *writ*." But in *Cobham* no such faith appears. On the contrary, Pope seeks to disabuse his readers of the notion that the "Principle of action" is the *vade mecum* that makes clear men's complex characters. Just as reason is not adequate to experience, principles, Pope argues, do not explain actions. In fact, reason appears powerless to read passionate human character correctly—for the same reason it cannot fully comprehend experience:

> On human actions reason tho' you can,
> It may be reason, but it is not man:
> His Principle of action once explore,
> That instant 'tis his Principle no more.
> Like following life thro' creatures you dissect,
> You lose it in the moment you detect.   [ll. 35-40]

That we ourselves often do not know what motivates us is further indication of the helplessness of a "Principle of action" to explain our behavior, which, Pope suggests, may be caused by deep and dark forces unknown to the consciousness:

> Oft in the Passions' wild rotation tost,
> Our spring of action to ourselves is lost:
> Tir'd, not determin'd, to the last we yield,
> And what comes then is master of the field.
> As the last image of that troubled heap,
> When Sense subsides, and Fancy sports in sleep,
> (Tho' past the recollection of the thought)
> Becomes the stuff of which our dream is wrought:
> Something as dim to our internal view,
> Is thus, perhaps, the cause of most we do.   [ll. 41-50]

For a number of reasons, then, it is foolhardy to expect to read the "why" in the "what." Pope's argument thus becomes a brief against intentionality. Our passionate, various, and mystifying behavior is, he insists, no reliable guide to intention.

> In vain the Sage, with retrospective eye,
> Would from th' apparent What conclude the Why,
> Infer the Motive from the Deed, and show,
> That what we chanc'd was what we meant to do.
> [ll. 51-54]

So many factors, conscious and unconscious, beyond our control as well as within it, enter into, influence, and even determine our actions that we cannot but conclude that they do not always "show the man" (l. 61). Indeed, writes Pope,

> we find
> Who does a kindness, is not therefore kind;
> Perhaps Prosperity becalm'd his breast,
> Perhaps the Wind just shifted from the east:
> Not therefore humble he who seeks retreat,
> Pride guides his steps, and bids him shun the great:
> Who combats bravely is not therefore brave,
> He dreads a death-bed like the meanest slave:
> Who reasons wisely is not therefore wise,
> His pride in Reas'ning, not in Acting lies.   [ll. 61-70]

The following verse paragraphs detail more specifics that influence our actions and frustrate our desire to find the key that unties the knot and "unravels all the rest" (l. 178). Though Pope is willing to grant that "Actions best discover man" (l. 71), he asks, "What will you do with such as disagree?" (l. 75). As he suggests elsewhere, contrary to our idealistic expectations, an important decision and subsequent action may hinge on arbitrary or quite mundane considerations: "Alas! in truth the man but chang'd his mind, / Perhaps was sick, in love, or had not din'd" (ll. 79–80). In such acknowledgments, Pope shatters a number of "realistic" notions concerning human action and character, apparently continuing the work of de-mythologization we noted in *An Essay on Man.*

And though he grants that we sometimes find "plain Characters" (l. 122), both those who "are open, and to all men known" and those who are "so very close, they're hid from none" (ll. 110-11), he concludes on the note he struck at the beginning of the poem: "Manners with Fortunes, Humours turn with Climes, / Tenets with Books, and Principles with Times" (ll. 166-67). Summing up his argument that change and difference are the principal characteristics of human conduct, Pope asks how, then, are we to read man, how to decide what is the truth about him:

> Judge we by Nature? Habit can efface,
> Int'rest o'ercome, or Policy take place:
> By Actions? those Uncertainty divides:
> By Passions? these Dissimulation hides:
> Opinions? they still take a wider range.   [ll. 168-72]

Perhaps recalling (aspects of) *An Essay on Man,* Pope's advice at this point seems not very reassuring: "Find, if you can, in what you cannot change" (l. 173).

"The only certain way to avoid Misconstruction"

Despite the obstacles and all the objections that we have noted, the unchangeable and unchanging is finally found (or, rather, posited). The unwobbling pivot, the clue that unties the knot and "unravels all," allowing—so Pope claims—for an accurate reading of human character, is the "ruling passion," an idea that Pope introduced in the second epistle of *An Essay on Man*. Whatever its limitations and deficiencies, the ruling passion has the advantage not available to those theories of reading dependent on conscious motivation and the de-mythologized notion of purposive action.

The ruling passion focuses Pope's reading of the enigmatic characters drawn after line 178 in the *Epistle to Cobham* and throughout the remaining *Moral Essays*. In it "alone," Pope declares in *Cobham*, "The Wild are constant, and the Cunning known; / The Fool consistent, and the False sincere; / Priests, Princes, Women, no dissemblers here" (ll. 174-77). The ruling passion is—to adopt Pope's phrasing from his address to Richard Boyle, Earl of Burlington, affixed to the fourth epistle—*"the only certain way to avoid Misconstruction."*

Pope tests the capacity of the ruling passion to reveal the truth about human behavior, making our conduct, in spite of its complexity and inconsistency, legible and clear. This he does in the second epistle by applying it to the "characters" of women, who are said to be even more various, inconsistent, and apparently incomprehensible than men. Indeed, opening *To a Lady*, Pope expresses agreement with Martha Blount that "'Most Women have no Characters at all'" (l. 2), being so changeable. Pope implies that if the ruling passion can provide a satisfactory reading of women, revealing order in the bewildering chaos that characterizes their actions, then it is a powerful and compelling theory, indeed. As it turns out, women prove easier to read than men, for whereas

In Men, we various Ruling Passions find,
In Women, two almost divide the kind;

> Those, only fix'd, they first or last obey,
> The Love of Pleasure, and the Love of Sway.
>
> [ll. 207-10]

In both men and women, the ruling passion functions like a controlling theme in a well-wrought literary text, toward which all the subordinate elements gravitate.

Differences, which (we thought) threaten to divide us irreparably, splitting us at least in two and making it perhaps impossible to think of a human being as a distinct entity with its own (proper) identity, are thus subsumed, in a sort of pre-Hegelian *Aufhebung*. Those differences are sublated in a transcendent unity capable of bestowing a recognizable and definite identity on individual men and women, after all. Pope offers not a little comfort in assuring us that we have "proper" characters, legible and distinct, and that this identity remains with us, until death:

> Time, that on all things lays his lenient hand,
> Yet tames not this; it sticks to our last sand.
> Consistent in our follies and our sins,
> Here honest Nature ends as she begins.
>
> [*Cobham*, ll. 224-27]

The pattern is the familiar one in Pope (as well as in the work of Pope scholars): after all is said and done and all the difficulties acknowledged, differences are reconciled, and harmony prevails where only discord had been apparent. Real identity triumphs over apparent difference, order prevailing in the world as well as in men and women, "All Chance [being in fact], Direction," and "All Discord, Harmony" (*An Essay on Man*, 1.290-91). All is well because all is being directed by "Th' Eternal Art educing good from ill" (ibid., 2.175). This "mightier Pow'r [than we] the strong direction sends, / And sev'ral Men impels to sev'ral ends" (ibid., 2.165-66). As the *Epistle to Bathurst* puts it, declaring that it is the truth about human character so earnestly sought though so often mistaken:

> Hear then the truth: "'Tis Heav'n each Passion
>   sends,
> "And diff'rent men directs to diff'rent ends.
> "Extremes in Nature equal good produce,
> "Extremes in Man concur to gen'ral use."
> Ask we what makes one keep, and one bestow?
> That Pow'r who bids the Ocean ebb and flow,
> Bids seed-time, harvest, equal course maintain,
> Thro' reconcil'd extremes of drought and rain,
> Builds Life on Death, on Change Duration founds,
> And gives th' eternal wheels to know their rounds.
>
> [ll. 161-70]

"A Standing Sermon"

Even aside from psychological and philosophical difficulties entailed in Pope's notion of the ruling passion,[6] the solution offered to the problem of reading human character in the *Moral Essays* appears unsatisfactory. As a theory of reading, it fails because it ignores the reader. That it ignores the reader is surprising since, early on in the *Epistle to Cobham*, as we saw, Pope urges us precisely not to forget the reader and the ways in which the reader inevitably affects what is read. Yet, in treating the ruling passion, Pope apparently forgets his own point, ignoring the reader's role in interpreting actions and in deciding which ruling passion is operative in a given individual. The ruling passion no more escapes the effects of the reader's imposition of his or her own opinions and passions than does the deflated notion of the "Principle of action." Pope's solution, then, is a solution only if we forget or ignore the earlier argument. It depends on an exclusion or, perhaps, on a hole.

What does this discovered lacuna in Pope's argument tell us? Is it an embarrassing story, revealing the poet's own inconsistency, contradictoriness, and even incompetence, and providing an odd parallel to the account given of human action? Is human action (like) a literary text, the self-difference (*différance*) they share indicating that both are writing? Might the revealed hole be filled by the (signifying) phallus that is the "whole"? That the hole exposed in Pope's argument, however, is more than a local instance of compositional error is indicated by the occurrence in Pope's text of what Barbara Johnson calls "a *systematic* 'other message' behind or through what is being said."

The *Moral Essays* offer declarations concerning this matter of unintentional stories being told through texts. In fact, they thematize the point. Such thematization occurs when, for example, in the *Epistle to Burlington* Pope writes that one "Prodigal" created through his extravagance his own "standing sermon." The passage ostensibly concerns the construction of a lavish and contemptible mansion, but it is also an allegory of reading:

> See! sportive fate, to punish aukward pride,
> Bids Bubo build, and sends him such a Guide:
> A standing sermon, at each year's expense,
> That never Coxcomb reach'd Magnificence!
>
> [ll. 19-22]

Designed as a thing of grandeur, the constructed edifice becomes a "standing sermon" because it is something other than, indeed contrary to, what was intended. Such recognition comes through reading against the grain.

Read in that manner, as Pope does, the prodigious struc-
ture functions as a sermon directed against prodigality.

What occurs in this passage is structurally identical to
what appears in the de-mythologizing of a "Principle of
action" as a reliable index to the characters of men and
women. It is also like the way in which God is said to turn
our activity to good, in spite of us and our intentions. Like
Pope, God is apparently something of a deconstructionist.
Just as Bubo's mansion becomes, in spite of his intentions,
"a standing sermon" on lavish and impractical expense,
and just as human conduct stems from motivation of
which we may not be conscious and occurs (sometimes)
as actions we never intended, so God goes against the
grain, subverting our intentions. "A standing sermon" is,
therefore, another name for that "*systematic* 'other mes-
sage'" appearing through the declaration.

In some other ways, too, Pope seems to anticipate Der-
rida, sounding deconstructive themes and assuming
deconstructive positions, for example depicting women
somewhat as the French philosopher does in *Spurs* and
even acknowledging that "by Man's oppression curst,"
women seek "the Love of Sway" so as not to lose "The
Love of Pleasure" (*To a Lady*, ll. 210-14).[7] But if this is so,
Pope certainly diverges at other points from anything ap-
proaching deconstruction. In addition to the implicitly
metaphysical and logocentric points we treated earlier (for
example, concerning reading), Pope explicitly supports
phallogocentrism and the primacy of the male, a position
we might not expect given his statement above that
women are oppressed by men; nevertheless, he writes to-
ward the end of *To a Lady:* "Heav'n, when it strives to
polish all it can / Its last best work, but forms a softer
Man" (ll. 271-72).

Moreover, though Pope insists on reading other-wise,[8]
contrary to apparent intentions and declarations, he

comes to rest as deconstruction never does. He stops, that is, with his inversion of the hierarchy that, for example, privileges Bubo's mansion as "Magnificence." Reversing the hierarchy, Pope himself insists that that structure is not at all "Magnificence" but simply a "standing sermon" *against* "Magnificence." He thus privileges the textual description at the expense of its explicit declarations. Though often considered merely destructive, deconstruction involves, as we have noted, a double gesture that does not rest content with hierarchical inversion, important as that "phase" is. Derrida goes to considerable lengths to make his "double science" clear, writing, for instance, in *Positions:* "To deconstruct the opposition, first of all, is to overturn the hierarchy at a given moment. . . . That being said—and on the other hand—to remain in this phase is still to operate on the terrain of and from within the deconstructed system. By means of this double, and precisely stratified, dislodged and dislodging, writing, we must also mark the interval between inversion, which brings low what was high, and the irruptive emergence of a new 'concept,' a concept that can no longer be, and never could be, included in the previous regime."[9] Deconstruction, that is, first intervenes in a violently maintained hierarchy, such as the man/woman "opposition," and proceeds to bring the superior "party" down, "momentarily" installing the "inferior" in its place. But far from ending with this inversion, it continues to operate, reinscribing in an interminable process of "reading" the newly elevated "term," subjecting it to the same deconstruction and ultimately producing a "new 'concept.'" Like the Bible, we might say, deconstruction refuses to let us rest comfortably in any place or position reached. Its target is the notion of hierarchization—its goal, the emergence of a new woman.[10]

Even if Pope is able to decide, to determine that the truth concerning, for example, Bubo's mansion is the simple contrary of that intended, his readers cannot easily do so. As readers, however, we do enjoy considerable power, as Pope has hinted (though he does not acknowledge that the recognition of a "standing sermon" is no less dependent on the reader than a straightforward, unsuspicious reading). But if the reader has power, he or she is not therefore in an enviable position. The reader of the *Moral Essays* is faced with two stories, intertwined, each with a "message" (part of which is that there is "a *systematic* 'other message' behind or through" what is being declared). Who shall decide between the two competing stories? We often cannot say that the poems, like Bubo's mansion, simply have "two meanings that exist side by side." The situation is far more problematical, as Paul de Man has written in another context: "The two readings have to engage each other in direct confrontation, for the one reading is precisely the error denounced by the other and has to be undone by it. Nor can we in any way make a valid decision as to which of the readings can be given priority over the other."[11]

And the point with which we began this section, concerning a satisfactory theory of reading? What we are left with is simply a *story of reading*. As unsatisfactory as it may appear to those who prefer to have matters neatly and clearly resolved, there are always texts *and* readers, reading being a dialogical activity characterized by—among other things—constant tension and a struggle of competing wills, as the reader's aforementioned drive toward univocity encounters the text's equally strong resistance.[12]

"Who Shall Decide?" The Economy of Truth in *An Epistle to Bathurst*

Of all Pope's poems, *An Epistle to Bathurst* may be said to offer the fullest treatment of the problem of deciding and the quest of truth that we have been considering. Complex and demanding, *Bathurst* explores the nature and economy of truth and the truth about some of our—and Pope's—most cherished truths. Though the poem has justifiably received considerable critical attention, the profound philosophical questions it raises and the perspectives it offers have not, I think, been adequately focused.[13]

In *Bathurst*, the longest of the *Moral Essays*, the economy of truth is inseparable from the truth of economy—or at least of money. Like the *Epistle to Burlington*, this poem focuses on "the use of riches." Pope's subject is gold and money, their usefulness, and human attitudes concerning them. Not so obvious perhaps but nonetheless crucial to the text's performance is the relation between money and truth. Exactly what that relation is, I want to explore, with considerable help from Marc Shell's recent studies *The Economy of Literature* and *Money, Language, and Thought*.[14]

Pope admits, somewhat grudgingly, that gold, considered as a medium of exchange, "serves what life requires" (l. 29). But because it panders to and indeed increases some of the baser human desires, gold has a negative as well as a positive aspect: "What Nature wants, commodious Gold bestows" (l. 21). Pope quickly adds, for a reason that I shall suggest below, that "What Nature wants" is "a phrase I much distrust" (l. 25). In Pope's view, in any case, a fundamental inequality and an unfairness reside in the exchange that gold makes possible: "'Tis thus we eat the bread another sows: / But how unequal it bestows, observe, / 'Tis thus we riot, while who sow it, starve" (ll. 22-24). Gold's influence, power, and capacity for significant abuse are simply "dreadful" to contemplate, for gold

> the dark Assassin hires:
> Trade it may help, Society extend;

But lures the Pyrate, and corrupts the Friend:
It raises Armies in a Nation's aid,
But bribes a Senate, and the Land's betray'd.

[ll. 30-34]

The coin has two sides, and Pope stresses the dark, negative side.

The major problem with gold, according to Pope, is precisely its capacity for advancing and spreading corruption; indeed, it facilitates both avarice and prodigality, and it creates falsehood and error. Better, then, Pope declares, if gold did not exist as a medium of exchange, for one can literally buy anything (material and otherwise) with it and sell anything for it. Better, in fact, if there were only the commodities themselves, as in former, less corrupt times, and perhaps an inconvenient but effective barter system for securing needed goods and services. Pope's account contains strong nostalgia for the simplicity and supposed virtue of a more pastoral existence that lacked the encouragement to vice gold offers:[15]

> Oh! that such bulky Bribes as all might see,
> Still, as of old, incumber'd Villainy!
> In vain may Heroes fight, and Patriots rave;
> If secret Gold saps on from knave to knave.
> Could France or Rome divert our brave designs,
> With all their brandies or with all their wines?
>
> . . . .
>
> Poor Avarice one torment more would find;
> Nor could Profusion squander all in kind.
> Astride his cheese Sir Morgan might we meet,
> And Worldly crying coals from street to street,
> (Whom with a wig so wild, and mien so maz'd,
> Pity mistakes for some poor tradesman craz'd).
> Had Colepepper's whole wealth been hops and hogs,
> Could he himself have sent it to the dogs?

His Grace will game: to White's a Bull be led,
With spurning heels and with a butting head.
To White's be carried, as to ancient games,
Fair Coursers, Vases, and alluring Dames.
Shall then Uxorio, if the stakes he sweep,
Bear home six Whores, and make his Lady weep?
Or soft Adonis, so perfum'd and fine,
Drive to St. James's a whole herd of swine?
[ll. 35-40, 47-62]

With the "progress" from gold coins to paper money, problems increase. Pope begins his diatribe with an echo of Proverbs 23:5, which condemns material wealth ("When your eyes light upon it, it is gone; for suddenly it takes to itself wings, flying like an eagle toward heaven"). Pope's account may remind us not only of the Paper Money Scene in *Faust* but also of the fierce debate concerning coined and paper money that dominated the American political scene for fifty years in the middle of the nineteenth century.[16]

Blest paper-credit! last and best supply!
That lends Corruption lighter wings to fly!
Gold imp'd by thee, can compass hardest things,
Can pocket States, can fetch or carry Kings;
A single leaf shall waft an Army o'er,
Or ship off Senates to a distant Shore;
A leaf, like Sibyl's, scatter to and fro
Our fates and fortunes, as the winds shall blow:
Pregnant with thousands flits the Scrap unseen,
And silent sells a King, or buys a Queen.   [ll. 69-78]

Paper money, even more than gold, facilitates secrecy, allowing error, vice, and sin to thrive. Throughout, Pope stresses the importance of this matter of visibility. As Marc Shell puts it, "In a monetary economy, invisible exchanges

. . . are easily effected. Not the presence of money but rather the absence of witness . . . makes such transactions 'invisible.'"[17] For Pope, gold is the virtual opposite of the sun, source of light and bearer of truth; it was (appropriately) buried and hidden "under ground" until brought out "by Man's audacious labour" (ll. 10-11). If gold is so bad, what can paper money, which is worse, signify?

According to Pope, paper money not only advances corruption and falsehood, but it is also itself false. Though gold is both commodity and coin, thing and symbol, paper money is simply a medium of exchange. Far from being "the thing itself," paper money is a representation of what is already a representation. Actually, Pope insists, gold is itself more—and worse—than a "mere" representation, for it comes to rival its sire, which Pope believed to be the sun's rays:

> Nature, as in duty bound,
> Deep hid the shining mischief under ground:
> But when by Man's audacious labour won,
> Flam'd forth this rival to, its Sire, the Sun.   [ll. 9-12]

In the family romance Pope tells, the son thus struggles with, and desires to usurp the place of, the father, the sun. In opposition stand the One (the sun) and the Money (the son).[18]

While lambasting gold and paper money as representations and therefore lies, Pope insists that truth is the thing itself: always visible, shining, and immediately available to everyone.[19] Anything hidden or not so accessible is false, as Pope establishes when, for example, he lashes those who "Some War, some Plague, or Famine . . . foresee, / Some Revelation hid from you and me" (ll. 115-16). A metaphysical stillness, truth is, in fact, like the sun, source of light: open, clear, and single. A thing is thus it-

self, proper, possessing uniqueness and identity; unequiv-
ocal, it is not also something else, a point Pope repeatedly
makes.

It may prove helpful to consider Pope's position in rela-
tion to what Shell writes about Plato's conception of truth:
for the philosopher, "the upward way . . . does not depend
finally on its opposite, the downward way. Plato pretends
that the etymology of *alētheia* (truth) is not 'the uncon-
cealed' but rather the unidirectional 'way of the god,'
which does not imply any negation."[20] Pope's declared po-
sition is obvious enough, but is he right? Or is truth per-
haps, like money, the unconcealed, as philosophers such
as Heraclitus and Heidegger believed, opposing the Pla-
tonic notion of the "unidirectional"? Pope believes, of
course, that what is unconcealed and brought from
"under ground" to light is not truth (*alētheia*) but its op-
posite. Must we choose between these two opposed posi-
tions, the sense of truth as approximation and that of un-
concealment? Might "truth" be inseparable from "not
truth"? Might it, in fact, be at the same time "not truth"?
If so, would "truth" be dialectical, in the way Shell sug-
gests?

"Who shall decide?" Pope asks in opening *Bathurst*.
Who, that is, will resolve, settle, answer clearly and deci-
sively, do the necessary cutting that the etymology of the
verb indicates that deciding involves and requires? Pope's
question is rhetorical, and according to Paul de Man's im-
portant analysis in "Semiology and Rhetoric," every rhe-
torical question cuts two ways and at once: whereas its
literal meaning insists on a specific response, its figurative
meaning implies the impossibility of deciding and con-
notes, indeed, some degree of resignation concerning this
fact.[21] Two equally possible but entirely incompatible ways
of reading Pope's *opening* question reside (uneasily) in the
question, which is itself addressed to a situation involving

two different, conflicting, and indeed incompatible re-
sponses. Pope's initial question opens out onto a difference
of opinion in the poem's two participants, Pope and his
addressee-interlocutor, the rakish Allen Lord Bathurst:

> Who shall decide, when Doctors disagree,
> And soundest Casuists doubt, like you and me?
> You hold the word, from Jove to Momus giv'n,
> That Man was made the standing jest of Heav'n;
> And Gold but sent to keep the fools in play,
> For some to heap, and some to throw away.   [ll. 1-6]

More optimistic than his friend (at least in this fiction),
Pope, who thinks "more highly of our kind, / (And surely,
Heav'n and I are of a mind)" (ll. 7-8), believes that Nature,
"as in duty bound," hid "the shining mischief" deep
"under ground." When man audaciously began to mine
gold and it came to rival its "sire," "careful Heav'n sup-
ply'd two sorts of Men, / To squander these, and those to
hide agen" (ll. 13-14). Each of the two accounts given,
that of Bathurst and that of Pope, is structured as a rec-
ognition of difference, indeed of polar opposition. But
since both participants in the discussion agree that some
heap gold while others squander it, what initially appears
a significant difference dissolves, prompting Pope to de-
clare, "Like Doctors thus, when much dispute has past, /
We find our tenets just the same at last" (ll. 15-16). No
decision is, then, necessary: what seemed to be difference
turns out to be actual identity. Such a resolution may sat-
isfy the literal meaning of the opening question, but what
about the figurative meaning, which implies the impossi-
bility of deciding?

And what of the structural pattern of which that impos-
ing initial question forms a part? Like *An Epistle to Dr.
Arbuthnot*, for example, *Bathurst* consists of a series of

differences, extremes, and polarities. Are they similarly dissolved? A recurring pattern in Pope involves the cancellation and ultimate transcendence of difference in an unexpected synthesis or unity. Elsewhere in *Bathurst*, certainly, difference dissolves. For example, picking up on the earlier point regarding the similarity of those who hide and those who squander gold, Pope asserts:

> Yet, to be just to these poor men of pelf,
> Each does but hate his Neighbour as himself:
> Damn'd to the Mines, an equal fate betides
> The Slave that digs it, and the Slave that hides.
>
> [ll. 109-12]

In a similar vein Pope later writes of the great and final destroyer of difference:

> Who builds a Church to God, and not to Fame,
> Will never mark the marble with his Name:
> Go, search it there, where to be born and die,
> Of rich and poor makes all the history.   [ll. 285-88]

These passages, like several others we remarked earlier, indicate that for Pope, no matter how complex truth is, it is finally one, difference being transcended and in fact transformed into an identity. Other passages in *Bathurst* appear, however, to drive a wedge into this univocal and monolithic understanding of truth. One of these is Pope's presentation of the fortuitously named Sir John Blunt, director of the infamous South Sea Company, in whose stock Pope unwisely invested. With apparent fidelity to the man, Pope first depicts Blunt as unscrupulous and hardhearted, the virtual opposite of the Man of Ross extolled later as the *imitatio Christi:* " 'God cannot love (says Blunt, with tearless eyes) / 'The wretch he starves'—and piously

denies" the poor (ll. 105-6). Pope's later, extended treat-
ment of Blunt, however, is complex and, I think, equivocal:

> Much injur'd Blunt! why bears he Britain's hate?
> A wizard told him in these words our fate:
> "At length Corruption, like a gen'ral flood,
> "(So long by watchful Ministers withstood)
> "Shall deluge all; and Av'rice creeping on,
> "Spread like a low-born mist, and blot the Sun;
> "Statesman and Patriot ply alike the stocks,
> "Peeress and Butler share alike the Box,
> "And Judges job, and Bishops bite the town,
> "And mighty Dukes pack cards for half a crown.
> "See Britain sunk in lucre's sordid charms,
> "And France reveng'd of ANNE's and EDWARD's arms!"
> No mean Court-badge, great Scriv'ner! fir'd thy brain,
> Nor lordly Luxury, nor City Gain:
> No, 'twas thy righteous end, asham'd to see
> Senates degen'rate, Patriots disagree,
> And nobly wishing Party-rage to cease,
> To buy both sides, and give thy Country peace.
>
> [ll. 135-52]

Among others, Earl Wasserman has ably discussed this
passage, observing how Pope's satire cuts two ways at
once: "The wizard's picture of corruption is valid, and
Pope can use the vision to lash at the current vice of riches.
But the corrupt Blunt . . . is not the man to inveigh against
them; a swindling Dissenter, he represents corruption
crying out against corruption with false piety and false
benevolence."[22] As I read it, no clear line exists in *Bath-
urst*'s treatment of Blunt to separate good absolutely from
bad. In terms of effects, there is a mixture of good and bad,
in Blunt perhaps a blunting of the truth.

Increasing the complexity of truth, and unsettling
Pope's sense of its economy, is supplementarity, which we

briefly discussed in connection with *An Essay on Man*. *Bathurst* thematizes supplementarity, just as it does difference. The poem is, in fact, full of supplements, of one kind or another. If Pope sometimes presents them negatively, as a fall from "the thing itself" (e.g., ll. 27-28 and 81-92, as well as a couplet I quoted earlier: "Blest papercredit! last and best supply! / That lends Corruption lighter wings to fly!"), at other times supplements are depicted as necessary and even good. This last point is perhaps clearest in relation to man's stewardship of riches (a steward is an *oikonomos*).[23] Whereas the wise and good steward will "ease, or emulate, the care of Heav'n" (l. 230), supplementing that work, others, including Blunt, as well as some clergymen, stubbornly and selfishly refuse to supplement:

> "God cannot love (says Blunt, with tearless eyes)
> "The wretch he starves"—and piously denies:
> But the good Bishop, with a meeker air,
> Admits, and leaves them, Providence's care.
>
> [ll. 104-7]

The fullest and most important account of supplementarity occurs in the depiction of the admirable John Kyrle, "The MAN of ROSS" (l. 250), "who with a small Estate actually performed all these good works" that Pope proceeds to detail.[24] Kyrle's outstanding characteristic is his acceptance of the relatedness that is our entry into humanity[25] and so of social responsibility, coupled with his work as steward of man's estate and supplement of "the care of Heav'n." In the opening verses of Pope's portrait, Kyrle appears God-like:

> Who hung with woods yon mountain's sultry brow?
> From the dry rock who bade the waters flow?

Not to the skies in useless columns tost,
Or in proud falls magnificently lost,
But clear and artless, pouring thro' the plain
Health to the sick, and solace to the swain.
Whose Cause-way parts the vale with shady rows?
Whose Seats the weary Traveller repose?
Who taught that heav'n-directed spire to rise?
[ll. 253-61]

The answer, the truth, is "The MAN of Ross, each lisping babe replies" (l. 262). In the following verses, Kyrle becomes unmistakably both an *imitatio Christi* and a *sequentia Christi:*

Behold the Market-place with poor o'erspread!
The MAN of Ross divides the weekly bread:
Behold yon Alms-house, neat, but void of state,
Where Age and Want sit smiling at the gate:
Him portion'd maids, apprentic'd orphans blest,
The young who labour, and the old who rest.
Is any sick? the MAN of Ross relieves,
Prescribes, attends, the med'cine makes, and gives.
[ll. 263-70]

The portrait concludes with verses depicting Kyrle as reconciler, peacemaker, and judge of differences, *deciding* disputes:

Is there a variance? enter but his door,
Balk'd are the Courts, and contest is no more.
Despairing Quacks with curses fled the place,
And vile Attornies, now an useless race.   [ll. 271-74]

In several ways, the Man of Ross thus emulates, represents, and supplements the work of Providence.

In presenting John Kyrle as a supplement of "the care

of Heav'n," Pope shows how this Christ-like figure *adds to* that effort. But as we have seen, a strange logic operates in supplementarity, and so far we have considered only a part of its work. Another part is more "dangerous," functioning as a substitution and not just an addition. Both these senses of the supplement appear in *Bathurst:* if "what Nature wants" (a phrase Pope admits that he much distrusts, l. 25) refers to what is lacking rather than what is desired, then gold as a supplement—or "supply," to use Pope's own repeated term—adds to, augments. But riches also function as a substitute—albeit a poor one—for what is truly needed:

> What Riches give us let us then enquire:
> Meat, Fire, and Cloaths. What more? Meat, Cloaths,
>   and Fire.
> . . . .
> What can they give? to dying Hopkins Heirs;
> To Chartres, Vigour; Japhet, Nose and Ears?
> Can they, in gems bid pallid Hippia glow,
> In Fulvia's buckle ease the throbs below,
> Or heal, old Narses, thy obscener ail,
> With all th' embroid'ry plaister'd at thy tail?
>   [ll. 81-82, 87-92]

Though Pope wants to keep these different, indeed conflicting senses of supplementarity distinct, "the shadow presence of the other meaning is always there to undermine the distinction."[26] Pope's third *Moral Essay* thus carries a double message: both a declaration, for example depicting Kyrle as simply an addition to the work of Providence, and a conflicting description that involves an ambivalent and equivocal presentation of the Man of Ross, much more complex than the structurally similar depiction of Sir John Blunt that we read earlier. Bodying forth the strange logic of supplementarity, John Kyrle not only emulates and eases the work of Providence, but he may also—in spite of "himself"—rival it and even take its place. Indeed, by means of that logic according to which, by Pope's own reckoning in *Bathurst* and elsewhere, good is educed from ill, Kyrle may undermine his own work and what he represents. Since, according to what I have described as God's deconstructive efforts, Providence uses individual and collective differences, directing them in ways we fallible and limited human beings cannot possibly know, in fact turning our actions in ways contrary to our willful intentions, then may not attempts to ease or emulate its work actually countermine that which they were intended to bring about? Perhaps, though, Providence is judiciously selective in its deconstruction, intervening in our bad actions so as to produce good in spite of ourselves, but gratefully accepting our good. In any case, something positive should be expected to come from those, like Blunt and "the good Bishop," who leave the poor completely to the care of Providence.

Whether or not Providence deconstructs our good actions as it does our evil, it apparently *requires* the labors of such direct supplementers as Kyrle. If it does, then it is hardly perfect. But as Pope presents Kyrle, *he* seems complete—and perfect—in himself. After all, he does everything himself, for example prescribing, making, and dispensing medicine. Kyrle appears, in short, to take the place of Providence, doing its work. Kyrle's own work, especially in its effectiveness, implies in Providence what Derrida calls "the anterior default of a presence." Needing the "supply" provided by people like the Man of Ross, Providence *lacks*, a void becoming apparent, another hole exposed. Because Providence requires human help just as humans ostensibly need its care and assistance, it evidently has to be supplemented.

In such a manner, *Bathurst* calls into question the notion of truth as univocal. Indeed, it *systematically* reveals the complex economy of truth, specifically its dialogical nature. This we begin to grasp via the oft-cited portrait of Balaam, with which Pope ends the poem. Balaam appears, even more than Blunt, as Kyrle's polar opposite; he is as Satanic as the Man of Ross is Christ-like. Whereas Kyrle accepted and enacted the responsibilities entailed in human relatedness, Balaam proudly and avariciously refuses to care, to help, to supplement. In fact, he effectively dislodges Providence as a force in his life, claiming self-sufficiency. Thus he "Ascribes his gettings to his parts and merit, / What late he call'd a Blessing, now was Wit, / And God's good Providence, a lucky Hit" (ll. 376-78). At the end, penniless, impeached, destitute, and alone, "sad Sir Balaam curses God and dies" (l. 402), shifting responsibility for his own manifold failures onto God, making Him a supplement of those failures.

Together, the Man of Ross, the *imitatio* and *sequentia Christi*, and Sir Balaam, who refuses to imitate the work of Providence, represent the two different and conflicting senses that Derrida has shown to co-exist in supplementarity. The two portraits constitute, in fact, an allegory of supplementarity. As we have seen, *Bathurst* declares that Kyrle adds to and therefore eases "the care of Heav'n" and that Balaam acts as a substitute, proudly refusing to acknowledge any power or force outside himself as responsible for his good fortune. But as the textual descriptions indicate, the logic of the supplement operates within this allegory of supplementarity, rending each of the two "poles," dividing each within. As a result, Kyrle, in Balaam-like self-sufficiency, becomes a rival of and substitute for Providence, much as gold comes to rival its sire the sun. Likewise, Balaam may be said to add to or advance the grand design of Heaven if, as Pope repeatedly assures us, the ill particular individuals do is ultimately directed, deconstructed, and transformed by a benevolent "Pow'r" into good for the whole.

Moreover, since Kyrle and Balaam each add to the *text*'s force and direction while rivaling each other, they function—beyond the thematic level at what might be called the material or textual level—as both additions to and substitutions for one another. The Man of Ross serves, of course, as the poem's ethical norm, a representation of its deeply Christian values, and ostensibly overshadows the evil Balaam represents, but the latter *is* powerfully presented, certainly memorable, and—whether or not more realistic—significantly accorded the final section. Kyrle and Balaam are described as exchanging places with one another, each being the battlefield between the warring forces that they (declaratively) represent as apparent opposites.

Other instances of the problematization of identity, and so of univocal truth, occur in *Bathurst*. There is, for example, the double meaning of the words I have quoted on more than one occasion: "What Nature wants." The verb means both to desire and to lack, the phrase being one (therefore?) that, Pope confesses, "I much distrust." Did Pope distrust the verb because it is untrustworthy, im-*proper*, equivocal? In any case, consider Pope's claim, also noted earlier, that the sun sired gold (l. 12), which is, therefore, the sun's son. We cannot but hear in this verse, as we did in *An Essay on Criticism*, both "sun" and "son," which illustrates the difference between *phonemes* and *graphemes*: as with the Derridean neologism *différance*, which is indistinguishable audibly from *différence*, so with "sun" and "son." About this situation Derrida writes:

The difference between two phonemes, which enables them to exist and to operate, is inaudible. The inaudible opens the two present phonemes to hearing, as they present themselves. . . .

The difference that brings out phonemes and lets them be heard and understood . . . itself remains inaudible. . . .

[Since] the difference between the *e* and the *a* marked in "difference" eludes . . . hearing, this happily suggests that we must here let ourselves be referred to an order that no longer refers to sensibility. But we are not referred to intelligibility either. . . . We must be referred to an order, then, that resists philosophy's founding opposition between the sensible and the intelligible. The order that resists this opposition, that resists it because it sustains it, is designated in a movement of differance (with an *a*) between two differences or between two letters. This differance belongs neither to the voice nor to writing in the ordinary sense, and it takes place . . . *between* speech and writing and beyond the tranquil familiarity that binds us to one and to the other, reassuring us sometimes in the illusion that they are two separate things.[27]

On this reading, which I have quoted at such length because of the way it brings together a number of points crucial to our exploration, the *a* of *différance* "remains silent, secret, and discreet, like a tomb"; it is a tomb, Derrida adds, that "is not far from signaling the death of the king."[28] The king is the sign, supposedly single, proper, and truth-ful. In *Bathurst*, to return at last to Pope, "sun" and "son" are brought together as their *différance*, and so we hear that the sun/son sired the son, which is then said to rival the sun. Does the son thus supplement the father, or does it supplement "itself," dividing "itself" within? "Who shall decide?"

The exchange (paying what sort of dividends, repaying how much interest?) between "sun" and "son" is paralleled by the blunt-ing of differences, and exchange, that occurs when, after the sun has been posited as (source of) truth, the figures traditionally associated with it are applied to a representation. Though early in *Bathurst* representation is treated, we recall, as falsehood, truth and representation are not opposed to each other in the following passage; on the contrary, copying is now roundly praised:

> Who copies Your's, or OXFORD's better part,
> To ease th' oppress'd, and raise the sinking heart?
> Where-e'er he shines, oh Fortune, gild the scene,
> And Angels guard him in the golden Mean!
>
> [ll. 243-46]

An Epistle to Bathurst thus describes, in a *systematic* manner, not only the collapse of absolute difference but also the impossibility of distinct identity and univocal truth. In this poem, Pope shows, descriptively, that a thing is and is not "itself." The point applies equally to the text that reveals this "truth." In its exploration of truth, *An Epistle to Bathurst* loses its own "identity."[29] As an allegory, it tells the story of the struggle between textual declaration and textual description. It also tells the story of two competing ideas of truth. One of these, deriving from Plato, holds that truth is, in Marc Shell's account, the "unidirectional 'way of the god,'" and the other posits truth as equivocal, indeed as dialogical, being inseparable from not-truth. This second notion of truth is related to, though it should be distinguished from, the Heraclitean and Heideggerian conception that Shell has presented. This latter conception is a dialectical one that regards truth as *alētheia*, the unconcealed.

We are dealing here, obviously, with both "truth" in general and the "truth" about Pope's poem. And though we should be sure not to confuse and identify the two pursuits, we must wonder about the relationship of these quests. Apparently in accord with the idea of truth as *alētheia*, the "truth" concerning *Bathurst* had to be "by Man's audacious labour won"; like gold, it had to be sought below the surface, where it lay hidden, and then brought to light, coming finally into unconcealedness. If I may pursue the analogy with gold, then the "truth" about *Bathurst* is both fathered by and will come to rival and eventually to replace that other (Platonic) conception of truth, associated with the sun (the father) and believed to be readily available. How can we be sure, in any case, that what we brought from concealedness to light, via reading, is the truth, any more than the traditional univocal reading? In short, is the deconstructive analysis of *Bathurst* "truer" than the other one? Actually, what the deconstruction makes clear, dependent on *Bathurst*'s complex explorations, is the connection, rivalry, and exchange that prevents us from resting with any possibility as the "truth," including any "truth" brought into unconcealedness. Our reading, deriving from the text's difficult lesson that truth is always on the move, reveals that truth is divided, dialogical, rather than unequivocal and univocal. Is that "truth" about "truth" "truer" than the deconstructed one? If truth is always on the move, and if reading seems to disillusion us, as the Bible does, concerning the possibility of a simple truth, exposing the untruthfulness of "truth," then the "truth" established by reading, even if posited as divided and dialogical, is no less logocentric and in need of further deconstruction. *Où reste . . . ?* Perhaps what matters is the use we make of what is taken as "truth." The use of riches.

ॐ Chapter Five

Becoming Woman

Writing, Self, and the Quest of Difference in the Imitations of Horace

Besides *An Essay on Man* and the *Moral Essays*, Pope's major poems of the 1730s are those we know by the rubric *Imitations of Horace*. This title is convenient but misleading—if not perverse—for only eleven of the seventeen poems included are more or less directly imitative of the Roman poet; the remaining poems include the two "imitations" of Donne, *An Epistle to Dr. Arbuthnot*, the two dialogues of the *Epilogue to the Satires*, and the fragment known as *One Thousand Seven Hundred and Forty*. If reading is the major concern in the *Moral Essays*, writing is the central thematic focus in these poems, which, despite some reservations, I follow the Twickenham Edition in calling *Imitations of Horace*. Several of these poems, in fact, deal centrally with the life of writing, though they do not exclude issues in reading; from *Arbuthnot*, often considered the prologue to this series of poems, to the *Epilogue to the Satires*, the *Imitations* focus on the social, political, and cultural state of writing, its value, and Pope's own *praxis*.

As these poems focus on the problem(atic)s of writing and its significance, they require considerable effort from the reader. By this I mean more than the recognition, no less accurate for being familiar, that Pope demands of his reader wide knowledge, close attention, and considerable skill in identifying and understanding the many allusions. That the reader of the *Imitations* becomes, in fact, a producer and not merely a consumer perhaps carries little surprise. After all, most of these poems are in some sense "about" their individual similarities to and differences from the Latin and English poems that they "imitate" and that Pope printed alongside his own texts. The reader of these poems is thus asked to relate and distinguish, part of his or her pleasure surely deriving from the ability to note both resemblance and difference. But that work, important as it is, is not all that Pope demands.

As the presence of the "imitated" poems alongside the "imitations" suggests, the work that Pope demands revolves around questions of difference. Especially since a number of critics have carefully and ably explicated the relation of Pope's to Horace's poems,[1] I shall concentrate on the ways in which difference functions as theme, goal, and strategy *within* the *Imitations*, without, I trust, neglecting the similarities to and differences from poems "imitated" wherever these bear on meaning. As Shakespeare does in Ulysses' famous speech on Order in the third act of *Troilus and Cressida*, Pope insists that distinction is the key to social and cultural survival, let alone excellence; without difference, as Pope goes on to claim in *The Dunciad*, light will be eliminated, "dread" chaos restored, and the "great Anarch" enthroned as ruler of all that is. As he lambastes Augustan society throughout the satires and epistles for its increasing failure to distinguish,

Pope tries, in and through his writing, to make a differ-
ence. This he does in part by requiring his reader to make
certain necessary distinctions.

In various ways, the *Imitations* require that the reader
exercise his or her ability to discriminate. *Sober Advice
from Horace*, "Imitated in the Manner of Mr. Pope," for
example, that apparent "jeu d'esprit" frequently called ob-
scene and pornographic,[2] has to do with the reader's re-
sponse to the value systems displayed in the verse by the
libertine "speaker" and in the mock notes by "Richard
Bentley," who thus reveal how they have responded to both
Horace and Pope. In *An Epistle to Dr. Arbuthnot*, the read-
er's responsibilities are different, extending beyond ques-
tions of Pope's intentions. What to make of this important
text, arguably the greatest of the *Imitations,* in which, im-
mediately after the devastating attack on Sporus, Pope
switches, without warning or apparent justification, to the
third person in referring to himself? Might this abrupt
change signal in him a recognition of the otherness within
"himself" and so perhaps the same self-difference he has
satirized in Sporus, "one vile Antithesis. / Amphibious
Thing!" (ll. 325-26)? Though the poem was evidently
constructed to persuade us that his own are "manly ways"
(l. 337), unlike Sporus's, Pope appears just as equivocal,
becoming clearly womanly by poem's end.

Whatever we make of the perplexing problems the *Im-
itations* present us with, questions of difference cannot be
avoided. Important among these questions is sexual dif-
ference. Obviously *Sober Advice* treats sex, but so does *Ar-
buthnot*, for example, even if this has rarely been recog-
nized. The latter poem especially makes clear the
inseparability of sex and writing. Given Pope's privileging
of man in *To a Lady* (woman comes after, being but "a
softer Man," l. 272), it is probably not surprising that he
considers writing a masculine activity. This is so at least

at the "level" of the declarations, his desire both to make a difference and to be different from the "plague" of poetasters exemplifying phallogocentrism. Textual description is, however, as always a different matter. The ways in which the male/female "opposition" structures Pope's exploration of writing, difference, and the self is one of my concerns in the pages that follow.

"Equivocation Will Undo Us"
"Adieu Distinction, Satire, Warmth, and Truth!"

No one has better discussed Pope's poetry in the 1730s than Maynard Mack, in *The Garden and the City: Retirement and Politics in the Later Poetry of Pope, 1731–43.*[3] Among Mack's contributions to our understanding of Pope, his poetry, and his milieu is his demonstration that the satirist used his "retirement" from the city as both opportunity and justification for the attacks he launched against King George II, the administration of Robert Walpole, and the art and morality they encouraged. Though Mack does not himself emphasize the term, we might say that Pope wants to make a difference, and his way of making a difference entails being different.

The first dialogue of the *Epilogue to the Satires*, published in 1738, summarizes what Pope found wrong in England in the 1730s: a pervasive eclipse of what *An Essay on Man* calls virtue. Pope's attack becomes as precise as it is emotionally heightened:

> See thronging Millions to the Pagod run,
> And offer Country, Parent, Wife, or Son!
> Hear [the] black Trumpet thro' the Land proclaim,
> That "Not to be corrupted is the Shame."

In Soldier, Churchman, Patriot, Man in Pow'r,
'Tis Av'rice all, Ambition is no more!
See, all our Nobles begging to be Slaves!
See, all our Fools aspiring to be Knaves!
The Wit of Cheats, the Courage of a Whore,
Are what ten thousand envy and adore.
All, all look up, with reverential Awe,
On Crimes that scape, or triumph o'er the Law:
While Truth, Worth, Wisdom, daily they decry—
"Nothing is Sacred now but Villany."   [ll. 157-70]

The themes sounded throughout the satires of the 1730s
appear here, including the inversion of values, "the Ava-
rice of Pow'r" (*Epistle* II.ii.307), the mad lust for gold, the
corruption of youth and the perversion of the nobility, and
the pervasiveness of slavery. All now being scorned "but
gold" (the second *Satire* of Donne, l. 24), charity and the
poor being neglected ("Oh Impudence of wealth! with all
thy store, / How dar'st thou let one worthy man be poor?"
[*Satire* II.ii.117-18]), the present age has simply bid
"Adieu [to] Distinction, Satire, Warmth, and Truth!" (first
dialogue of the *Epilogue to the Satires*, l. 64).

Preeminently among the poems of the 1730s, *Epistle*
II.i. (*To Augustus*) makes this loss of the ability to distin-
guish its central concern. Maintaining that this condition
characterizes the nobility no less than the "Mobs," Pope
argues that indiscrimination in literary taste and loss of
critical judgment presage collapse of social distinction.

What dear delight to Britons Farce affords!
Farce once the taste of Mobs, but now of Lords;
(For Taste, eternal wanderer, now flies
From heads to ears, and now from ears to eyes.)
The Play stands still; damn action and discourse,

> Back fly the scenes, and enter foot and horse;
> Pageants on pageants, in long order drawn,
> Peers, Heralds, Bishops, Ermin, Gold, and Lawn;
> The Champion too! and, to complete the jest,
> Old Edward's Armour beams on Cibber's breast!
> With laughter sure Democritus had dy'd,
> Had he beheld an Audience gape so wide.
> Let Bear or Elephant be e'er so white,
> The people, sure, the people are the sight!
> Ah luckless Poet! stretch thy lungs and roar,
> That Bear or Elephant shall heed thee more;
> While all its throats the Gallery extends,
> And all the Thunder of the Pit ascends!
> Loud as the Wolves on Orcas' stormy steep,
> Howl to the roarings of the Northern deep.
> Such is the shout, the long-applauding note,
> At Quin's high plume, or Oldfield's petticoat,
> Or when from Court a birth-day suit bestow'd
> Sinks the lost Actor in the tawdry load.
> Booth enters—hark! the Universal Peal!
> "But has he spoken?" Not a syllable.
> "What shook the stage, and made the people stare?"
> Cato's long Wig, flowr'd gown, and lacquer'd chair.
>
> [ll. 310-37]

In this situation, attention is misdirected, values all askew, the outside being privileged: of interest is the spectacle alone, the outward trappings, what the eye can see, what does not require interpretive or critical effort.

At least partly responsible for this situation, according to Pope, is bad writing, and one reason why writing is now bad is that everyone, talented or not, seems driven to write: "those who cannot write, and those who can, / All ryme, and scrawl, and scribble, to a man" (*Augustus*, ll. 187-88). Like *Arbuthnot* (e.g., "All *Bedlam*, or *Parnassus*, is let out: / Fire in each eye, and Papers in each hand, /

They rave, recite, and madden round the land," ll. 4-6),
Augustus claims that

>   one Poetick Itch
> Has seiz'd the Court and City, Poor and Rich:
> Sons, Sires, and Grandsires, all will wear the Bays,
> Our Wives read Milton, and our Daughters Plays,
> To Theatres, and to Rehearsals throng,
> And all our Grace at Table is a Song.
> . . . .
> When, sick of Muse, our follies we deplore,
> And promise our best Friends to ryme no more;
> We wake next morning in a raging Fit,
> And call for Pen and Ink to show our Wit.
>   [ll. 169-74, 177-80]

Given the lust for gold and "the Avarice of Pow'r," of
which writers are by no means innocent, Englishmen
have, says Pope in various poems, given themselves to flat-
tery, in an effort to enlist the rich and powerful in advanc-
ing their own selfish causes: "The Poets learn'd to please,
and not to wound: / Most warp'd to Flatt'ry's side" (*Au-
gustus*, ll. 258-59). As a result, "Satire is no more—I feel
it die" (*Epilogue to the Satires*, Dialogue I.83). What satire
does exist, Pope claims, is mere libel. Much—if not
most—of the blame for this deplorable situation rests, ac-
cording to Pope, with the King, the Court, and the Wal-
pole administration, for whom the current "Poetick Itch"
is propitious: allow the crazed scribbler "but his Play-
thing of a Pen, / He ne'er rebels, or plots, like other men"
(*Augustus*, ll. 193-94). Moreover, neither the King nor his
Court *can* distinguish sufficiently to support the worthy
and deserving. Because George Augustus cannot distin-
guish, Pope asserts in *Epistle* II.i., flatterers are promoted.
And because the King cannot make the necessary distinc-

tions, Pope can write this particular poem, ostensibly praising him but actually satirizing him. Pope gambles that the king will not be able to negotiate the double meanings of his verse nor discern the uncompromising satire. As he slyly writes, "Kings in Wit may want discerning spirit" (l. 385). *To Augustus* thus becomes a particular kind of satirical performance, demonstrating George the reader's inability to distinguish.

A somewhat similar situation (as well as strategy) obtains in *Sober Advice from Horace,* also addressed to the loss of critical judgment. I have argued elsewhere that, just as Pope impersonates Bentley in the pedantic notes to the English poem, so he creates a completely fictional "speaker," specifically a Restoration rake, who offers an imitation of Pope imitating Horace.[4] At least part of the point, with both "Bentley" and the rakish *persona,* is the nature of their (undiscriminating) response to both poets. Though superficially quite different, their responses are actually similar. Whereas the literal-minded "Bentley" is obsessed with technical accuracy in rendering the *words* of Horace and oblivious to meanings and effects,[5] the poem's "speaker," interested only in "God's good Thing" (l. 103), undermines poetic and moral values in giving free rein to man's baser, animalistic instincts and indeed in using poetry to glorify them. Such an effort dissipates the satirical force of the Horatian *sermo* as the satirized *persona* either misunderstands the texts on which he draws or else willfully transforms them for his own libidinous purposes. How the reader responds to this sermon promoting fornication, as well as to the mock notes, matters greatly. We might say, in fact, that the poem reads the reader. Pope clearly expects his reader to make distinctions that neither "Bentley" nor the rakish *persona,* like George Augustus, is able to make. In dramatizing such inability to distinguish, Pope works to make a difference.

Pursuing Difference

Pope's (vain but no doubt sincere) commitment is to something like the green world dreamed of in Shakespearean romance.[6] Even if such cannot be realized in Augustan England, he tries to effect some difference in the way things are. For him to do so, he believes, he must be and appear different. In a number of respects, of course, including physical, religious, and intellectual, he *was* different. The epistles and satires we are now treating he constructs as complex and carefully orchestrated attempts to establish definitively his difference from the corruption of City and Court, from the pervasive literary and cultural indiscrimination, and from the "plague" of poetasters hounding him wherever he goes.

The strategy involves, first of all, physical separation and geographical distance. *The Fourth Satire of Dr. John Donne, Dean of St. Paul's, Versify'd* dramatizes Pope's imagined experiences at Court, depicting both the villainy he hates and the distance from it he desires:

> Bear me, some God! oh quickly bear me hence
> To wholesome Solitude, the Nurse of Sense:
> Where Contemplation prunes her ruffled Wings,
> And the free Soul looks down to pity Kings.
>
> [ll. 184-87]

If he is to write, Pope claims, he must get away from London, for "Who there his Muse, or Self, or Soul attends? / In Crouds and Courts, Law, Business, Feasts and Friends?" (*Epistle* II.ii.90-91). The apparent answer to this desire of physical distance is, of course, Pope's cherished "retreat" at Twickenham, where he can be properly contemplative and attend to the stirrings of his heart. His opposition of city and country parallels that familiar in Fielding's novels as well as elsewhere in the period.

> Soon as I enter at my Country door,
> My Mind resumes the thread it dropt before;
> Thoughts, which at Hyde-Park-Corner I forgot,
> Meet and rejoin me, in the pensive Grott.
> There all alone, and Compliments apart,
> I ask these sober questions of my Heart.
>
> [*Epistle* II.ii.206-11]

Unfortunately for Pope, even Twickenham does not provide the difference sought, as *An Epistle to Dr. Arbuthnot* makes abundantly clear. The "undistinguish'd race" (l. 237) of "Witlings" invade even this sacred "retreat": "All fly to *Twit'nam,* and in humble strain / Apply to me, to keep them mad or vain" (ll. 21-22). As the poem opens, Pope cries to his servant, "Shut, shut the door, good *John!* fatigu'd I said, / Tye up the knocker, say I'm sick, I'm dead." Sequestering and protecting himself from the "Plague" (l. 29) raging outside, Pope thus dramatizes the desire for literary and moral difference that lies at the heart of this poem. Widely used as a symbol for loss of distinction, the metaphor of plague functions, according to René Girard, as a "generic label for a variety of ills that . . . threaten or seem to threaten the very existence of social life."[7] Faced with such threats, Pope preserves his difference not only by escaping from the poetasters but also by carefully establishing his difference from those who lack discrimination and sufficient difference.

"Let Us be fix'd, and our own Masters still"

What distinguishes Pope from "the Race that write," the ubiquitous and avaricious flatterers, and the literary and political sycophants is in part his independence. "Thanks to *Homer*," he proudly declares, referring, of course, to the money he earned on the translation, he is "Indebted to no Prince or Peer alive" (*Epistle* II.ii.69–70). His financial security allows for intellectual, moral, and literary independence: "No Pimp of Pleasure, and no Spy of State" (*Satire* II.i.134), "Sworn to no Master, of no Sect am I" (*Epistle* I.i.24). As a result, Pope claims to be objective, interested only in virtue, no matter where it is found:

> I follow *Virtue*, where she shines, I praise,
> Point she to Priest or Elder, Whig or Tory,
> Or round a Quaker's Beaver cast a Glory.
> . . . .
> To find an honest man, I beat about,
> And love him, court him, praise him, in or out.
> [*Epilogue to the Satires*, Dialogue II.95-97, 102-3]

He is thus different from those driven by desire for fame, praise, and glory, who are subject to continuous buffeting:

> O you! whom Vanity's light bark conveys
> On Fame's mad voyage by the wind of Praise;
> With what a shifting gale your course you ply;
> For ever sunk too low, or born too high!
> Who pants for glory finds but short repose,
> A breath revives him, or a breath o'erthrows!
> [*Augustus*, ll. 296-301]

Closely related to Pope's proud and fierce independence is his constancy and singleness of purpose, unlike the wild changeableness of the flatterers and sycophants. Their lust and avarice produces, as Dante understood, constant movement, the opposite of the contemplativeness Twickenham symbolizes: "If Wealth alone then make and keep us blest, / Still, still be getting, never, never rest" (*Epistle*

I.vi.95-96). As Pope suggests (see, for example, *Epistle* I.i.41 and *Epistle* II.ii.73), such inconstancy at least threatens loss of self. Certainly it produces equivocalness: in their quest of gold, power, and place, their success being dependent on others, the greedy have to become what is expected of them and to be what those holding the keys to "success" want them to be. Unlike the (supposedly) univocal Pope, dependent on no one, the avaricious become all things to all men, losing any sense of distinct identity. For himself and those he cares about, Pope's wish is appropriately simple: "Let Lands and Houses have what Lords they will, / Let Us be fix'd, and our own Masters still" (*Satire* II.ii.179-80). "Equivocation will undo us."

Exposing Himself in the "impartial Glass"

Such is the context of the life of writing that Pope describes as his calling in the *Imitations of Horace*. Though many of these poems treat in a significant way the subject of writing, *Satire* II.i. (*To Fortescue*) will serve to introduce and focus the issues with which we need to be concerned. Later in this chapter I shall devote individual sections to *Augustus, Sober Advice,* and *Arbuthnot.*

In *Fortescue*, reiterating his independence and objectivity ("Un-plac'd, un-pension'd, no Man's Heir, or Slave," l. 116), Pope avers that "To VIRTUE ONLY and HER FRIENDS" is he (as well as his writing) "A FRIEND" (l. 121). He further declares himself an instrument of truth, asserting that he will conceal or hold back nothing but instead will tell the truth, even if it is unflattering to himself and his friends. Like them, he will appear naked, exposed in the truly reflecting mirror of his satire. An expression of Pope's continuing privileging of the inside, his claim recalls *An Essay on Criticism.*

I love to pour out all myself, as plain
As downright *Shippen*, or as old *Montagne.*
In them, as certain to be lov'd as seen,
The Soul stood forth, nor kept a Thought within;
In me what Spots (for Spots I have) appear,
Will prove at least the Medium must be clear.
In this impartial Glass, my Muse intends
Fair to expose myself, my Foes, my Friends;
Publish the present Age, but where my Text
Is Vice too high, reserve it for the next:
My Foes shall wish my Life a longer date,
And ev'ry Friend the less lament my Fate.   [ll. 51-62]⁸

For Pope's reader this conception of the particular na-
ture of virtue and truth may well create certain difficul-
ties. Pope's intention is to be strictly impartial: he holds that
truth lies on and with no side or "part." Believing in what
he terms "moderation," Pope may be misunderstood,
however, as favoring one side or another or both, indis-
criminately, even equivocally.

My Head and Heart thus flowing thro' my Quill,
Verse-man or Prose-man, term me which you will,
Papist or Protestant, or both between,
Like good *Erasmus* in an honest Mean,
In Moderation placing all my Glory,
While Tories call me Whig, and Whigs a Tory.
                                        [ll. 63-68]

Both the need for and the difficulty of distinction is ap-
parent when we juxtapose this passage and the following
lines from *To Augustus*, which lash inconstancy:

Britain, changeful as a Child at play,
Now calls in Princes, and now turns away.
Now Whig, now Tory, what we lov'd we hate;

> Now all for Pleasure, now for Church and State;
> Now for Prerogative, and now for Laws;
> Effects unhappy! from a Noble Cause.   [ll. 155-60]

The truth, though, is by now familiar: rather than equiv-
ocate, or oscillate from side to side, Pope actually rises
above and transcends individual differences (so the story
goes), residing in the "truth" that is one even if never seen
whole by the various partisans. Pope's claim is thus to the
same holistic vision he prizes in *An Essay on Criticism* and
in *An Essay on Man.* The point is amplified in *Epistle* I.i.:

> Sworn to no Master, of no Sect am I:
> As drives the storm, at any door I knock,
> And house with Montagne now, or now with Lock.
> Sometimes a Patriot, active in debate,
> Mix with the World, and battle for the State,
> Free as young Lyttelton, her cause pursue,
> Still true to Virtue, and as warm as true:
> Sometimes, with Aristippus, or St. Paul,
> Indulge my Candor, and grow all to all;
> Back to my native Moderation slide,
> And win my way by yielding to the tyde.   [ll. 24-34]

Pope's freedom and candor must, then, be distinguished
from the changeableness and equivocation that he de-
plores. Such discrimination proves hard work for the
reader, particularly as Pope's stance involves ironies,
tones, and strategies sometimes easily misunderstood.
The most important consequence of the difficulty in read-
ing Pope is the burden placed on the reader, whose own
ability to distinguish is actively called into play and fre-
quently tested rather severely.

Double Reading *To Augustus*
Framing the King

Earlier I commented on some of the ways in which *Augustus* focuses on the widespread inability to distinguish, for example satirizing the king for his lack of the "discerning spirit" needed to read that poem correctly. Complicating the problem, if not creating it, for both George Augustus and Pope's other readers past and present, is the presence of irony, particularly in the political "frame" surrounding the discussion of the condition and value of poetry. Irony always entails, of course, questions of intention and necessitates a double reading since what is being overtly declared is not what is meant. Though there is obviously some resemblance, this situation is by no means identical to the declaration/description that characterizes the double movement of deconstruction. In irony, both overt and "real" (i.e., satirical) meanings derive from authorial intention; in deconstruction, on the other hand, what I have been calling description derives from the textual play of language. To those being satirized via irony, only overt meanings should appear. In the case of *Augustus*, this is the fulsome praise of the king, "flattered" by the poem's "speaker" as profusely as by those Pope elsewhere satirizes. To those of us blessed, as the king was not, with some "discerning spirit," the meaning appears double, as Pope evidently intended it. The overt meaning (the praise) is, however, strictly a function of, indeed is subordinate to and undercut by, the satire.

From the opening lines we are invited to read ironically the ostensible praise of George II. This we can, and will, do if we possess certain minimal information and are attuned to the doubleness of Pope's procedure. If he or she is to read these verses ironically, the reader may need to know, for example, that English ships were routinely being harassed at sea and that George Augustus spent much of his time in the arms of his German mistress. If the reader happens to share Pope's *interpretation* that the king could not be credited with advancing the cause of the arts, morality, or good government, all the better. Such shared knowledge, or interpretation, certainly assists the reader, and it may even be necessary for an ironical reading. But the possibility of doubleness inherent in the words themselves should not be neglected.[9] I think Irvin Ehrenpreis correct in writing that these lines "may be read as either eulogy or vituperation."[10]

> While You, great Patron[11] of Mankind, sustain
> The balanc'd World, and open all the Main;
> Your Country, chief, in Arms abroad defend,
> At home, with Morals, Arts, and Laws amend;
> How shall the Muse, from such a Monarch, steal
> An hour, and not defraud the Publick Weal?   [ll. 1-6]

Even if we are entitled to say—thanks to historical and biographical information as well as to the entire tradition of reading the poem—that Pope's intentions are (apparently) clear, we must grant that *Augustus* "works" only if such lines as I have quoted may also be read as straightforward praise, however saccharine.

By the end of the poem, when Pope returns to the king, completing the "frame," the irony appears somewhat more complicated yet also more obvious. Pope works to ensure that his reader read double. As a matter of fact, he has already stated unequivocally (albeit ironically) that he lies: "I, who so oft renounce the Muses, lye, / Not——'s self e'er tells more *Fibs* than I" (ll. 175-76). At the close, he even suggests, in acknowledging that what he "aims" as praise actually satirizes, that his efforts undercut—de-construct—themselves.

> Not with such Majesty, such bold relief,
> The Forms august of King, or conqu'ring Chief,
> E'er swell'd on Marble; as in Verse have shin'd
> (In polish'd Verse) the Manners and the Mind.
> Oh! could I mount on the Mæonian wing,
> Your Arms, your Actions, your Repose to sing!
> What seas you travers'd! and what fields you fought!
> Your Country's Peace, how oft, how dearly bought!
> How barb'rous rage subsided at your word,
> And Nations wonder'd while they dropp'd the sword!
> How, when you nodded, o'er the land and deep,
> Peace stole her wing, and wrapt the world in sleep;
> Till Earth's extremes your mediation own,
> And Asia's Tyrants tremble at your Throne—
> But Verse alas! your Majesty disdains;
> And I'm not us'd to Panegyric strains:
> The Zeal of Fools offends at any time,
> But most of all, the Zeal of Fools in ryme.
> Besides, a fate attends on all I write,
> That when I aim at praise, they say I bite.
> A vile Encomium doubly ridicules;
> There's nothing blackens like the ink of fools;
> If true, a woful likeness, and if lyes,
> "Praise undeserv'd is scandal in disguise:"
> Well may he blush, who gives it, or receives;
> And when I flatter, let my dirty leaves
> (Like Journals, Odes, and such forgotten things
> As Eusden, Philips, Settle, writ of Kings)
> Cloath spice, line trunks, or flutt'ring in a row,
> Befringe the rails of Bedlam and Sohoe.   [ll. 390-419]

Within the rather obvious irony is a tantalizing inconsist-ency in the "I." If the "I" of line 415 is straightforwardly Pope, that at lines 408-9, as at lines 175-76, is ironic.

"Discerning spirit" may be necessary to detect the difference, but the difference helps lead the reader to Pope's declared intentions.

"Know[ing] the Poet from the Man of Rymes"

If the opening and closing verses "frame" George Augustus, ostensibly lavishing him with the praise he wants to hear but actually satirizing him for his lack of "discerning spirit," indeed convicting him for that failure, the "inside" centers on the value of writing, whose complexity the frame well establishes. (That the relationship of frame to thing framed is not unproblematical is just the point, politics and writing being obviously interimplicated.) In both situations, the focus is on the ability to distinguish. The frame centers on the king's lack of critical judgment, precisely what it requires of the reader, and the rest of the poem, like *An Essay on Criticism*, offers its own exact discriminations and critical assessments, in the process establishing the grounds for true distinction.

Part of the problem Pope treats, and must cope with strategically, is that George II is popular: he frequently received such praise as Pope only ironically gives. That situation opens Pope's argument for the need of discrimination. Immediately after asserting that "Suns of Glory please not till they set" (l. 22—still another play on "sun" and "son"), Pope turns to George Augustus and declares, without *pointing to* the difference, that *he* already pleases: "To Thee, the World its present homage pays, / The Harvest early, but mature the Praise" (ll. 23-24). Pope adds a few lines later that his subjects are "partial" to George: "Foes to all living worth except your own" (ll. 32-33). Pope thus draws a significant difference that the reader must recognize, a difference "the people" do not make.

They simply cannot distinguish good from bad, true from false, whether the subject be the king or authors ancient and modern:

> Authors, like Coins, grow dear as they grow old;
> It is the rust we value, not the gold.
> Chaucer's worst ribaldry is learn'd by rote,
> And beastly Skelton Heads of Houses quote.
>
> [ll. 35-38]

In authors, what matters to the public is "staying power," or reputation over a period of time; the irrational claim, in fact, is that "'Who lasts a Century can have no flaw'" (l. 55). Partial to older writers, as they are to the king, Pope's contemporaries, so he claims, censure works "not as bad, but new; / While if our Elders break all Reason's laws, / These fools demand not Pardon, but Applause" (ll. 116-18). If one dare ask whether Shakespeare has any flaws, or criticize the actors Betterton and Booth, "How will our Fathers rise up in a rage, / And swear, all shame is lost in George's Age" (ll. 125-26). Pope's double-edged point here is, of course, that, though the age does lack shame, it is not for the reasons adduced by such critics.

As he had defined "the true critic" in *An Essay on Criticism*, so in *Augustus* Pope proceeds to offer a description of the true poet. This description immediately follows the long passage I quoted earlier (ll. 310-37) concerning the *translatio* of indiscrimination from City to Court, from "Mobs" to "Lords." Different from those who are, in every sense, undistinguished, undistinguishing, and indeed undistinguishable, the true poet, declares Pope, is he who can affect and move the reader or spectator, appealing to his or her innermost being:

> Let me for once presume t'instruct the times,
> To know the Poet from the Man of Rymes:

> 'Tis He, who gives my breast a thousand pains,
> Can make me feel each Passion that he feigns,
> Inrage, compose, with more than magic Art,
> With Pity, and with Terror, tear my heart;
> And snatch me, o'er the earth, or thro' the air,
> To Thebes, to Athens, when he will, and where.
>
> [ll. 340-47]

That Pope's primary concern, like that of classical and Renaissance criticism, lies in a text's *effects* and impact on an audience is apparent in a number of ways. It appears, for example, in his interest in George Augustus as reader, including as reader of the poem Pope is writing. In *To Augustus*, moreover, as in *Sober Advice from Horace*, Pope exhibits the effects on himself of his reading of Horace's "original" poem, of which the English version constitutes a response and an interpretation. As he indicates in the "Advertisement" to *Augustus*, Pope is especially interested in the *application* of Horace to the situation in Augustan England; that is, he uses the Horatian poem to interpret the present: "The Reflections of *Horace*, and the Judgments past in his Epistle to *Augustus*, seem'd so seasonable to the present Times, that I could not help applying them to the use of my own Country" (I reverse italics and roman). For Pope, imitation presupposes application and use, the aim being elucidation of the present (rather than antiquarianism or historicism, satirized, in fact, in the reader responses dramatized in *Sober Advice*). As Joel Weinsheimer has written in an insightful essay on imitation and the question of application in hermeneutics, "the end of interpretation, if it includes application, is self-knowledge. What true literature is foremost true of, is the interpreter."[12]

What Pope has done with Horace he expects his reader to repeat with him—not necessarily to write an imitation interpreting his poem but at least to respond to it, to open himself or herself to it so as to be involved in it in important ways and affected by it. Especially because the passage eliciting my comments treats the drama, I am reminded of Stephen Booth's recent—and apposite—discussion of "indefinition" in Shakespearean tragedy. Discussing the way we work to make tragedy (which is by definition the undefinable) bearable, Booth claims that "it is in the interest of human comfort to insist that dramatic tragedy happens on the stage and not in the audience, where the only real action of a play must necessarily occur."[13] Pope agrees, and he extends the principle to his own efforts in *To Augustus,* the important action of that poem occurring in the reader. Pope is, in the terms he uses, therefore a "Poet."

"Rely[ing] / More on a Reader's sense, than Gazer's Eye"

From the verses quoted above (ll. 340-47), Pope proceeds to urge the king to "Think of those Authors . . . who would rely / More on a Reader's sense, than Gazer's eye" (ll. 350-51). His point is directed against the current privileging of the trappings, the outside, what an actor wears at the expense of the part acted and of the lines spoken. Lines 310-37, quoted earlier, roundly criticize this situation: "(For Taste, eternal wanderer, now flies / From heads to ears, and now from ears to eyes)" (ll. 312-13). As manifested in the distinction drawn between "the Poet" and "the Man of Rymes," Pope's interest, characteristically, is with what happens inside, to the reader or spectator.

In order to establish its central point concerning the need to distinguish, *To Augustus* enacts what Pope talks about in lines 350-51: in a number of specific ways, the poem "rel[ies] / . . . on [the] Reader's Sense." Unless, in fact, the reader is able to distinguish as neither George Augustus nor "the Publick" can, the poem makes little sense, several important passages appearing an indiscriminate mess of often-conflicting opinions and contradictory judgments—in short, striking instances of the very equivocation Pope elsewhere repudiates. To a far greater extent than any other poem we have so far considered, *To Augustus* makes the reader a *producer* of its meaning, actively involving him or her in the construction of its meaning, finally depending on him for its most important effects. Though it is sometimes confused with "affective aesthetics," such a strategy as Pope's in *Augustus* is principally concerned with the "Reader's sense"; it is, therefore, more cognitive than affective, though affectivity is certainly involved. Whatever the degree of cognition and affectivity, the focus is on what happens inside the reader.

As I claimed earlier, *To Augustus* is constructed around the notion (and recognition) of difference. We have, in fact, already remarked some instances of this construction: the double meanings at work in the praise of George II, the difference between the king's popularity and the "Suns of Glory" who "please not till they set," and the necessity of valuing writers for "the gold" rather than "the rust." Especially when he praises the present and criticizes the so-called "classick," Pope may seem differentiating in the sense of *partial*. If he is, then he obviously flouts his assertions elsewhere concerning objectivity and impartiality. Yet he also *praises* the past, invoking it as the standard by which the present is assessed and, in so many ways, found lacking. Pope thus seems, as he declares, to "grow all to all," Moderns calling him Ancient, Ancients calling him Modern. Is he, therefore, equivocal, no matter what he claims?

Actually, Pope only *seems* to "grow all to all." The reason for the possible misreading is that his (declared) judgment is frequently double (though not equivocal or contradictory), as in the following passage, which requires that the reader do the work of making the assessments for which the passage merely presents the opportunity:

> Tho' justly Greece her eldest sons admires,
> Why should not we be wiser than our Sires?
> In ev'ry publick Virtue we excell,
> We build, we paint, we sing, we dance as well,
> And learned Athens to our Art must stoop,
> Could she behold us tumbling thro' a hoop.
>
> [ll. 43-48]

These verses suggest a notable range of attitudes: the first couplet is a rhetorical question the answer to which is both obvious and reasonable; the second begins to modulate away from celebration of present achievements toward the bathetic judgment of the final line. Rather than consistent irony, this short passage exemplifies the both/and stance Ehrenpreis locates in the poem's panegyric *and* vituperative frame. There is, in short, both straightforward and legitimate praise *and* biting satire, and the reader's job consists of recognizing the justness of both. In a certain sense, such a passage reads the reader, implicating him in the satire lashing the inability to distinguish if he takes either a partial or an equivocal position, *either* monolithically condemning the past or present *or* failing to note the different values implied.

As he proceeds, Pope dramatizes the inability to distinguish that he finds to be a characteristic of his age. Such lines as I just quoted suggest that he does not share that inability, though they depend on the reader for that perception. But whereas Pope shows "discerning spirit," for example praising Shakespeare while granting that "the divine, the matchless" poet "For gain, not glory, wing'd his roving flight, / And grew Immortal in his own de-spight" (ll. 70-72), an undiscriminating contemporary asserts, monolithically:

> "Yet surely, surely, these were famous men!
> "What Boy but hears the sayings of old Ben?
> "In all debates where Criticks bear a part,
> "Not one but nods, and talks of Johnson's Art,
> "Of Shakespear's Nature, and of Cowley's Wit;
> "How Beaumont's Judgment check'd what Fletcher
>   writ;
> "How Shadwell hasty, Wycherly was slow;
> "But, for the Passions, Southern sure and Rowe.
> "These, only these, support the crouded stage,
> "From eldest Heywood down to Cibber's age.
>   [ll. 79-88]

The wildly wrong judgment of Shadwell and Wycherley prompts a note from Pope, clarifying and correcting this assessment: "Nothing was less true than this particular: But the whole Paragraph has a mixture of Irony, and must not altogether be taken for Horace's own Judgment, only the common Chatt of the pretenders to Criticism; in some things right, in others wrong." Succeeding lines in the poem stress the point and dramatize the proper attitude, focused impartially on value:

> . . . . the People's Voice is odd,
> It is, and it is not, the voice of God.
> To Gammer Gurton if it give the bays,
> And yet deny the Careless Husband praise,
> Or say our fathers never broke a rule;
> Why then I say, the Publick is a fool.
> But let them own, that greater faults than we
> They had, and greater Virtues, I'll agree.   [ll. 89-96]

In going on to cite the case of Milton, Pope further exemplifies the proper complexity of judgment, which grants to the writer of *Paradise Lost* and *Areopagitica* both sublimity and bathos, recognizing, therefore, that he is not "of a piece": Pope distinguishes this double-edged judgment from Bentley's monolithic and undiscriminating criticism, rebuked in *Sober Advice* and *The Dunciad* as well:

> Milton's strong pinion now not Heav'n can bound,
> Now serpent-like, in prose he sweeps the ground,
> In Quibbles, Angel and Archangel join,
> And God the Father turns a School-Divine.
> Not that I'd lop the Beauties from his book,
> Like slashing Bentley with his desp'rate Hook;
> Or damn all Shakespear, like th' affected fool
> At Court, who hates whate'er he read at School.
>
> [ll. 99-106]

Though a number of other passages as well invoke the reader's "discerning spirit," requiring judgment that the verses themselves do not explicitly make (e.g., ll. 282ff.), the reader's most extensive labor probably comes in working through the long passage in which Pope attempts to persuade George Augustus that "a Poet's of some weight, / And (tho' no Soldier) useful to the State" (ll. 203-4). This important verse paragraph, which is a mélange of wildly divergent values and judgments, opens with Pope's assertion, cited earlier, that writing serves as a useful diversionary strategy for corrupt courts and governments, becoming a "Play-thing" that keeps men's attention away from public and political matters. Pope then describes the function of poetry in mundane terms as—if not a trifle—certainly an instrument of relatively mean value:

> What will a Child learn sooner than a song?
> What better teach a Foreigner the tongue?

> What's long or short, each accent where to place,
> And speak in publick with some sort of grace.
>
> [ll. 205-8]

After declaring that "In all Charles's days" not even Dryden could boast "unspotted Bays" (ll. 213-14), Pope turns to the current scene of writing, offering first a panegyric on Addison, whom he attacks as Atticus in *An Epistle to Dr. Arbuthnot:*

> And in our own (excuse some Courtly stains)
> No whiter page than Addison remains.
> He, from the taste obscene reclaims our Youth,
> And sets the Passions on the side of Truth;
> Forms the soft bosom with the gentlest art,
> And pours each human Virtue in the heart.
>
> [ll. 215-20]

Following this account of poetry's moral function and civilizing capacity comes a ringing tribute to Pope's friend Swift, which asserts writing's political opportunities, responsibilities, and achievements—in short, its way of making a difference. Pope's modulating description of writing's power and function climaxes here:

> Let Ireland tell, how Wit upheld her cause,
> Her Trade supported, and supply'd her Laws;
> And leave on SWIFT this grateful verse ingrav'd,
> The Rights a Court attack'd, a Poet sav'd.
> Behold the hand that wrought a Nation's cure,
> Stretch'd to relieve the Idiot and the Poor,
> Proud Vice to brand, or injur'd Worth adorn,
> And stretch the Ray to Ages yet unborn.   [ll. 221-28]

I shall pause over this heroic passage long enough to note the "presence" of "the strange logic of the supplement"—tracing of which entails considerable work for the reader. By means of the verb "supply'd," cognate to "supplemented," the passage, which recalls that on the Man of Ross in *An Epistle to Bathurst*, states *both* that Swift's writing added to or assisted Ireland's laws *and* that it came to substitute for them. Forcefully asserting writing's grave responsibilities, these lines claim that "The Rights a Court attack'd, a Poet sav'd." To preserve these rights, writing had to "supply" the country's laws, making up "for [their] deficiencies," to use the Twickenham Edition gloss on that verb. The two different meanings of "supply'd" engage each other in endless conflict, and the reader is unable to choose decisively between them; the meaning of the verb as a substitute deconstructs its meaning as an addition and vice versa, in ceaseless oscillation.

Immediately following the dramatic lines on Swift come verses offering a strikingly different account of poetry and its value, an account that harks back to the mundane description at the beginning of the paragraph. The lines in question begin with praise of Sternhold and Hopkins, translators of the Psalms and frequent butts of satire for their (at best) bad rhymes. What is striking is not only that they are treated in the same breath as Swift but also that no distinction is suggested regarding their very different value. The effect is to place them on the same level with Swift. But again, I suggest, with these verses as well as those that follow, Pope's reader must *supply* the necessary distinctions:

> Not but there are, who merit other palms;
> Hopkins and Sternhold glad the heart with Psalms;
> The Boys and Girls whom Charity maintains,
> Implore your help in these pathetic [!] strains:
> How could Devotion touch the country pews,
> Unless the Gods bestow'd a proper Muse?

> Verse chears their leisure, Verse assists their work,
> Verse prays for Peace, or sings down [Alexander?] Pope
>   and Turk.
> The silenc'd Preacher yields to potent strain,
> And feels that grace his pray'r besought in vain,
> The blessing thrills thro' all the lab'ring throng,
> And Heav'n is won by violence of Song.   [ll. 229-40]

Ending with such double meanings as I have marked with brackets, this entire verse paragraph is, whether or not read as reflecting the judgment of a single and consistent *persona*, ironic or straight, a definitely mixed bag. But we fail to do justice to Pope's strategy if we focus on the "speaker's" opinions, which in fact are so mixed that we cannot find any consistency in that "speaking voice." What Pope is really interested in is the *reader's* efforts to sort through and differentiate the varying implied judgments, "in some things right, in others wrong." The paragraph precisely calls the reader to *supplement* those judgments: that is, both to add to them and to substitute for them when they appear wrong. In *Augustus* to a far greater extent than in the other poems we have considered by Pope, the reader is invoked as a *supplement* of the text's (apparent) declarations. Here, in other words, Pope intends that the reader do at least part of what we ventured to do elsewhere without his sanction and blessing.

Sober Advice from Horace
Screwing Around

In such cases as *To Augustus* and *Sober Advice from Horace*, despite our stubborn humanistic mystifications, it may be irony that creates the illusion of a "speaking voice" belonging to an existent "speaker" who stands behind his statements as creator and guarantor of their meaning; we persist in believing, however, that a "speaker" is responsible for irony, endowing the human agent with the power properly belonging to this trope. Of course, as J. Hillis Miller has recently written concerning the novel, whether or not the text is an ironic one there is "the illusion of the character of the narrator. The narrator seems to be a man (or woman) speaking to men (or women)"; there is, moreover, Miller adds, "an almost irresistible temptation to think of the narrative voice as that of the author himself."[14] But irony is a special instance of the situation Miller describes, one closer, in fact, to Roland Barthes's famous remarks on "the death of the author": "Linguistically, the author is never more than the instance writing, just as *I* is nothing other than the instance saying *I*: language knows a 'subject', not a 'person', and this subject, empty outside of the very enunciation which defines it, suffices to make language 'hold together.'"[15]

In *To Augustus*, the play of irony creates the illusion that a "speaker" (i.e., Pope) "speaks" straightforwardly in declaring "when I flatter, let my dirty leaves / . . . / Cloath spice, line trunks, or flutt'ring in a row, / Befringe the rails of Bedlam and Sohoe" but that that "speaker" does not mean what he "says" when he asserts, "I, who so oft renounce the Muses, lye, / Not——'s self e'er tells more *Fibs* than I." In Pope's version of Horace's early *Satire* I.ii., on the other hand, the irony is not local but ubiquitous. At a more comprehensive level than *To Augustus*, *Sober Advice* invokes the reader's labor, turning him or her into an active producer of the poem's meaning by asking him to supplement *all* the "speaker's" declarations.

As I mentioned earlier, I have argued elsewhere that the fictional "speaker" of *Sober Advice* is *identifiable* as—indeed possesses the identity, the oneness, of—a Restoration rake "living" in Augustan England. I shall not rehearse my various arguments in support of this claim. I shall simply point out that the "speaker" everywhere alludes to personalities and events of the Restoration, exhibits the interests and values we associate with that period (from the drama to smut), and praises other rakes as he flouts morality, in the process transforming Horace's *satire* into *praise* and advocacy of fornication.

Thus with a playfully perverse echo of the Bible as well as a striking misappropriation of Pope's own themes and attitudes, the "speaker" asks:

> Hath not indulgent Nature spread a Feast,
> And giv'n enough for Man, enough for Beast?
> But Man corrupt, perverse in all his ways,
> In search of Vanities from Nature strays:
> Yea, tho' the Blessing's more than he can use,
> Shun the permitted, the forbid pursues!
> Weigh well the Cause from whence these Evils spring,
> 'Tis in thyself, and not in God's good Thing:
> Then, lest Repentence punish such a Life,
> Never, ah, never! kiss thy Neighbour's Wife.
>
> [ll. 96-105]

Rather than risk all the trouble and dangers that adultery may produce (the last several verse paragraphs graphically describe some of these), one should accept the feast kindly spread by Nature and in fact blessed by "My Lord of L——n," who

> chancing to remark
> A *noted Dean* much busy'd in the Park,
> "Proceed (he cry'd) proceed, my Reverend Brother,
> "'Tis *Fornicatio simplex*, and no other:

"Better than lust for Boys, with *Pope* [Alexander?] and
   Turk,
"Or others Spouses, like my Lord of——   [ll. 39-44]

Sober Advice is constructed as "a sermon against adul-
tery" (the title of the poem's 1738 reissue) and as a pane-
gyric on "indulgent Nature" and the "Feast" she kindly
spreads (for men). It is directed against the obstinate and
"unnatural" insistence that only "a Dame of Quality" (l.
70) will satisfy. In a witty variation (and perversion) of the
Pauline theme that, though "containment" is preferable
to marriage, "it is better to marry than to be aflame with
passion" (1 Cor. 7:9), the "speaker" asks:

Has Nature set no bounds to wild Desire?
No Sense to guide, no Reason to enquire,
What solid Happiness, what empty Pride?
And what is best indulg'd, or best deny'd?
If neither Gems adorn, nor Silver tip
The flowing Bowl, will you not wet your Lip?
When sharp with Hunger, scorn you to be fed,
Except on *Pea-Chicks*, at the *Bedford-head?*
Or, when a tight, neat Girl, will serve the Turn,
In errant Pride continue stiff, and burn?
I'm a plain Man, whose Maxim is profest,
"The Thing at hand is of all Things the *best.*
                        [ll. 143-54]

What the "speaker" reveals throughout this poem con-
structed of such *double entendres* is a libertine and amoral
response to both Horace and Pope, whose imitation of the
former the rake himself "imitates." The poem's meaning
thus centers in the "speaker's" imitation of these poets—
and in *our* interpretation of *his* response. Our job, in fact,
is to recognize "his" failures and perversions for what they
are and to judge them accordingly. We must, then, *supple-*

ment "his" declarations. But whether we do or not, *Sober Advice from Horace* reads us.

Getting into "the Thing," or the Part and the Hole

If, from the opening discussion of misers and spendthrifts to the focus several lines later on "the hackneyed theme of the grave and quite unnecessary risks involved in adultery with women of society,"[16] Horace proceeds in a casual manner befitting the conversational pattern of urbane men speaking to one another, the situation is different in *Sober Advice*. It opens with the subject that almost obsessively occupies its attention throughout: women and sex. Instead of a beginning contrast between miserliness and prodigality, the extremes in *Sober Advice* are female generosity with "God's good Thing" (l. 103) and feminine avarice resulting in the use and abuse of sex. Having stated his "Theme" ("'Women and Fools are always in Extreme,'" ll. 27-28), Pope's "speaker" proceeds with a graphic description of women that in coarseness goes well beyond Horace:

> *Rufa*'s at either end a Common-Shoar,
> Sweet *Moll* and *Jack* are Civet-Cat and Boar:
> Nothing in Nature is so lewd as *Peg*,
> Yet, for the World, she would not shew her Leg!
> While bashful *Jenny*, ev'n at Morning-Prayer,
> Spreads her Fore-Buttocks to the Navel bare.
> But diff'rent Taste in diff'rent Men prevails,
> And one is fired by Heads, and one by Tails;
> Some feel no Flames but at the *Court* or *Ball*,
> And others hunt white Aprons in the *Mall*. [ll. 29-38]

Whereas Horace frequently seems interested in shocking, the rakish "speaker" of *Sober Advice* is more involved, in-

sinuating, and arousing. Indeed, he expands on possibili-
ties mainly latent in the Latin poem, turning the occa-
sional bluntness into extended metaphors less like the
double entendres of Restoration comedy than the "pornog-
raphy" of Rochester's "obscene" verses:

> Suppose that honest Part that rules us all,
> Should rise, and say—"Sir *Robert!* or Sir *Paul!*
> "Did I demand, in my most vig'rous hour,
> "A Thing descended from the Conqueror?
> "Or when my pulse beat highest, ask for any
> "Such Nicety, as Lady or Lord *Fanny?*—
> What would you answer? Could you have the Face,
> When the poor Suff'rer humbly mourn'd his Case,
> To cry "You weep the Favours of her GRACE?
>
> [ll. 87-95]

Despite the strikingly different contexts, this passage re-
calls Pope's persistent concern with the parts-whole prob-
lem. The significance of the relationship these lines hint
at becomes clearer when we link parts-whole with the in-
side/outside opposition that also figures prominently in
Pope's poetry from *An Essay on Criticism* on. In *Sober Ad-
vice*, of course, like everything else inside/outside is
fraught with heavily sexual overtones. As a matter of fact,
just preceding the lines I quoted is a blunt passage treat-
ing "*Ellis*" and his desire "to be where CHARLES had been
before" (ll. 81-82). After declaring that "his Pride" led to
punishment by "The fatal Steel" (ll. 83-84), Pope's
"speaker" concludes: "Too hard a Penance [!] for defeated
Sin, / Himself shut out, and *Jacob Hall* let in" (ll. 85-86).
"That honest Part" being the phallus, the whole to which
that part seeks to relate is here the female hole. Is the
parts-whole issue, like the outside/inside opposition,
therefore a sexual allegory?

For Pope, as we have seen, the inside is frequently privileged, and in *Sober Advice from Horace* the goal of all (masculine) activity is the "Thing" (l. 90), indeed "God's good Thing," the "speaker's" "private" view being that "'The Thing at hand is of all Things the *best*" (l. 153). Pope too has not only consistently privileged the inside, but he has also sought to reach—in whatever sense—"the thing itself." Is "the thing itself" therefore "God's good Thing"? Is the whole to which Pope has always tried to relate the hole to which he wants entrance? Provocative possibilities.

Textual Play and Sexual Difference

Certainly, *Sober Advice from Horace* is sexist, raucously so, in fact. Even if the poem was designed by the poet as I have argued, with a consistently fictional—and thoroughly satirized—*persona* distinct from Pope and created via irony, and if, therefore, Pope maintains (and wishes his readers to take) a critical attitude towards this dirty "sermon," its wit, humor, and fun cannot be denied, at least not by males. I suspect that Pope, who prided himself on his "manly ways" (*Arbuthnot*, l. 337), delighted in the scurrilous wit even as he transformed it into a moralistic "statement" dependent on the reader's judgment. I expect that female readers are considerably less titillated: if not by the sly dirty jokes themselves, they are probably offended by the marginalization that the poem imposes upon women, relegated to sexual "objects" and dehumanized. Perhaps in terms of our gender as well as our attitudes, *Sober Advice* reads *us*. In any case, the seriousness that I have argued for cannot be separated from the dirty fun that is not cancelled out by the overarching moral intentions. The situation is reminiscent of that in *An Essay on Criticism*.

Whether or not my speculations concerning a relationship between matters sexual and Pope's perennial interest in parts-whole and inside/outside have any validity, the quest for "the thing itself," as Derrida suggests in *Spurs*, is clearly a masculine drive. There is no doubt that *Sober Advice*, understood as the "speaker's" poem, is phallogocentric, literalizing masculine desire for conquest and mastery and subjugating the female. But if the drive is masculine, the "object" sought, "the Thing," the truth quested for, the inside that the outside always wants, is feminine. Perhaps nowhere in the poem do these points converge as they do in the following verses, describing the quest of "God's good Thing," depicted as surrounded and protected by numerous obstacles trying to keep the inside safe and intact from the threatened invasion outside. The quest for the naked truth is determined, however.

> A Lady's Face is all you see undress'd;
> (For none but Lady M—— shows the Rest)
> But if to Charms more latent you pretend,
> What Lines encompass, and what Works defend!
> Dangers on Dangers! obstacles by dozens!
> Spies, Guardians, Guests, old Women, Aunts, and
>   Cozens!
> Could you directly to her Person go,
> Stays will obstruct above, and Hoops below,
> And if the Dame says yes, the Dress says no.
> Not thus at *N—dh—m*'s; your judicious Eye
> May measure there the Breast, the Hip, the Thigh!
>
> [ll. 123-34]

What would this truth unveiled as woman (naked) look like? If it *is* feminine, as Pope suggests perhaps in spite of himself, exactly *how* is it feminine? Is it intact and inviolate, or might it be always already not-inviolate? Like the "easy" women at "*N—dh—m*'s"? Scandalous possibility, truly, one that suggests an added dimension to the quest of truth in *An Epistle to Bathurst.*

What, in any case, about writing? Have I not lost sight of it amid all the talk of wit and sexuality and Pope? Perhaps writing is like truth. Perhaps, as I suggested earlier, there is more to writing than our narrow sense suggests. This other, larger sense of writing is that revealed to us by Jacques Derrida as the structure of difference marked by the trace. On this understanding, writing is inclusive, with apparently nothing escaping textuality.

An Epistle to Dr. Arbuthnot
Feminizing Pope

Earlier in this chapter, I contended that the subject of *An Epistle to Dr. Arbuthnot* is Pope's desire for literary and moral difference from the "plague" of poetasters who accost him whenever he ventures from Twickenham. That they even invade his "retreat" there prompts his opening exclamation to his servant, "Shut, shut the door, good *John!* fatigu'd I said, / Tye up the knocker, say I'm sick, I'm dead" (ll. 1-2). Dramatically presented here, Pope's desire for separation, distance, and difference is masculine. That this is so appears not only in the phallic symbolism of the second line but also in Pope's quest, detailed in the poem, as well as elsewhere, for absolute distinctions and definite truth, simple, clear, and univocal. That quest is inseparable from the desire of mastery (which the satirized "speaker" of *Sober Advice from Horace* shares) as well as the desire to be distinct and to possess a clear identity. From the outset, Pope wants to establish what he terms his "manly ways" (l. 337), absolutely different from the inadequately masculine Atticus, the feminized Bufo, and the indeterminate, undecidable Sporus, the latter "one vile Antithesis. / Amphibious Thing!" (ll. 325-26).

Often regarded as Pope's *apologia pro satura sua, An Epistle to Dr. Arbuthnot* depicts writing, in unmistakably sexual terms, as distinctly masculine, thus matching Pope's own desires. Indeed, Pope describes his own writing in explicitly sexual terms as offering the satisfaction a partner wants and expects: "The Muse but serv'd to ease some Friend, not Wife" (l. 131). The sexuality of writing appears, too, when Pope notes that "ev'ry Coxcomb knows me by my *Style*" (l. 282), "*Style*" suggesting not only the *Stylus* but also (therefore) the penis. The references to Gildon's "venal quill" (l. 151), to Bufo "puff'd by ev'ry quill" (l. 232), and to "each gray goose quill" that a patron may "bless" (l. 249), as well as to "slashing *Bentley*" (l. 164), further link pen to penis. According to Freud, we might recall, writing (in the narrow sense, pre-typewriter and -word processor) consists of "making a liquid flow out of a tube onto a piece of white paper," thereby assuming "the significance of copulation."[17] With his pen(is), the writer seeks pen-etration. *Arbuthnot* is a remarkable allegory of writing as copulation.

As Pope develops his defense of himself and his writing, it is "the Race that write" (l. 219) that emerges as the masculine force, one that sexually threatens him, in fact. Seeking to escape from them, Pope appears, contrary to his desire, as feminine (I adopt provisionally, putting it under erasure, Pope's own stereotypical and oppositional view of sexual difference). Indeed, he is feminized, or at the very least threatened with feminization, by the aspiring writers. If the poem's opening couplet is phallic, succeeding verses, with even clearer sexual symbolism, present Pope in the role of woman: for example, "What Walls can guard me, or what Shades can hide? / They pierce my

Thickets, thro' my Grot they glide" (ll. 7-8). To return for a moment to the concerns that marked the close of our consideration of *Sober Advice from Horace*, writing is, then, more than simple graphic inscription; it is, according to *Arbuthnot*'s declarations, penetration of and copulation with a woman. If *Arbuthnot* is, as I suggested above, an allegory of writing as copulation, is *Sober Advice* an allegory of copulation as writing?

In any case, in *Arbuthnot*, courted by the "Witlings," Pope is the sexual object whom these writers pursue. This structure establishes not only the masculine nature of writing as Pope declares it but also the feminine nature of the response sought by writers, who want a patron. That a patron, such as the poetasters hope to find in Pope, is feminized appears most clearly in the famous portrait of Bufo. In this portrait, arguably the most important difference Pope tries to make in *Arbuthnot*, Pope aims to distinguish himself from the false friend (and ultimately foe) that the patron is. Bufo's importance in the poem, however, derives as well from his similarity to Pope, particularly in being courted by the flattering poetasters.

> Proud, as *Apollo* on his forked hill,
> Sate full-blown *Bufo*, puff'd by ev'ry quill;
> Fed with soft Dedication all day long,
> *Horace* and he went hand in hand in song.
> His Library, (where Busts of Poets dead
> And a true *Pindar* stood without a head)
> Receiv'd of Wits an undistinguish'd race,
> Who first his Judgment ask'd, and then a Place:
> Much they extoll'd his Pictures, much his Seat,
> And flatter'd ev'ry day, and some days eat:
> Till grown more frugal in his riper days,
> He pay'd some Bards with Port, and some with Praise,
> To some a dry Rehearsal was assign'd,
> And others (harder still) he pay'd in kind.

Dryden alone (what wonder?) came not nigh,
Dryden alone escap'd this judging eye:
But still the Great have kindness in reserve,
He help'd to bury whom he help'd to starve.

[ll. 231-48]

According to this portrait, what Pope feared does happen
to a patron: "puff'd by ev'ry quill," Bufo has imposed upon
him the role of woman in "hosting" the would-be poets.
This is precisely what Pope rejects: he refuses to grant the
poetasters satisfaction, declining to "copulate" with them,
to be either their reader or their sponsor, refusing the role
of woman they would impose upon him—and succeed in
imposing upon Bufo.

But this is only part of the story, which, like all stories,
has a perhaps surprising turn. For Bufo (at least) has his
revenge on the emasculating writers: he becomes the cas-
trated yet castrating woman. In his library (or womb) lie
"dead" poets. Are these poets merely "spent," having been
satisfied, or is it that, feminized, Bufo feminizes the fem-
inizers, turning (masculine) writers into females if they
are given their way?

Here it may help to consider the portrait's thematic fo-
cus on parasite-host relations, an analogue of flatterer-
flattered. Clearly, the "plague" of poetasters surrounding
Bufo, like "the Race that write" courting Pope, are para-
sites. By means of this structure, the portrait dramatizes
the turning of one thing into another that I have already
mentioned. This transformation destabilizes differences
arrested as oppositions. In a well-known essay that I have
cited before, J. Hillis Miller has traced the etymology of
the terms "host" and "parasite" and has shown how, far
from being the opposites that we commonly suppose, they
are interimplicated, each always already containing a
"trace" of "the other" within "itself."[18] This of course fur-

ther problematizes the distinction between inside and outside. In *Arbuthnot*, the patron-flattered-host Bufo, like the "vain Patron" mentioned in *An Essay on Man*, functions as flattered-parasite vis-à-vis those who initially appear as parasite-poetasters, for if as host Bufo *feeds* the "undistinguish'd race" of "Wits," he *feeds* in turn *on* the very parasites he feeds, changing places with them, in fact turning into one of them, in a wild and dizzying "see-saw between *that* and *this*" (l. 323). As a result, he is just as "undistinguish'd" as they are and indeed identifiable as neither simply parasite nor host, flatterer nor flattered, man nor woman but, in all cases, as both.

Becoming what "she hates and ridicules"

Somewhat like Bufo, Pope combines in himself masculine and feminine traits (at least as Pope presents these, they are stereotypical and opposed), in spite of his desire for "manly ways." This feminization occurs, as we have seen, in the act of withdrawing himself from the "Witlings" (that that act is also one of separation and differentiation and therefore "masculine" is a complication I shall consider below). By poem's end, many more feminine qualities appear in Pope. In addition to two changes I have already remarked (the notable change of tone as well as the abrupt shift to third person in referring to himself, beginning at line 334), there is an important difference in attitude. What emerges is nothing less than a split in both poem and poet, and that split is, in the final analysis, precisely what constitutes woman. I follow Derrida, who writes in *Spurs* that "the 'woman' is not a determinable identity. Perhaps," he continues, "woman—a non-identity, a non-figure, a simulacrum—is distance's very chasm, the out-distancing of distance, the interval's cadence, distance itself, if we could still say such a thing, distance *itself.*" In short, "There is no such thing as the essence of woman because woman averts, she is averted of herself. . . . There is no such thing as the truth of woman, but it is because of that abyssal divergence of the truth, because that untruth is 'truth.'" Thus: "Woman is but one name for that untruth of truth."[19] Writing becomes woman, as does truth.

The difference in *An Epistle to Dr. Arbuthnot* and in Pope emerges most clearly as Pope praises his deceased father and his infirm mother for their tolerance and forbearance.[20] As the son develops the brief but effective account of his parents, the reader cannot but notice, it seems to me, the strong difference implied. Whereas the poet rather easily condemned others and launched often scathing attacks, his "Father held it for a rule / It was a Sin to call our Neighbour Fool, / That harmless Mother thought no Wife a Whore" (ll. 382-84). To be sure, such passages are designed to show the injustice, as well as the gross insensitivity, of the attacks on the poet's family, but the effects can by no means be limited to such intentions. In fact, the following portrait of the elder Pope develops the implied differences between father and son, becoming a clear criticism of the poet as he has appeared in such passages as the verses on Atticus, Bufo, and Sporus (more on this last directly). Presented as something of a hero, the elder Pope even receives the epithet the poet had hoped for and sought: "The good Man." Unlike the son, moreover, the father never let himself become involved in civil or religious controversy, never offered a "Bill of Complaint," the phrase Pope uses in the "Advertisement" to describe his own efforts in *Arbuthnot,* and never tried a "Suit," as Pope does in a number of the *Imitations.* In phrases that inevitably recall his earlier descriptions of "this long Disease, my Life" (l. 132), Pope contrasts his own physical deformity and proneness to illness with his father's lifelong good health:

> Born to no Pride, inheriting no Strife,
> Nor marrying Discord in a Noble Wife,
> Stranger to Civil and Religious Rage,
> The good Man walk'd innoxious thro' his Age.
> No Courts he saw, no Suits would ever try,
> Nor dar'd an Oath, nor hazarded a Lye:
> Un-learn'd, he knew no Schoolman's subtle Art,
> No Language, but the Language of the Heart.
> By Nature honest, by Experience wise,
> Healthy by Temp'rance and by Exercise:
> His Life, tho' long, to sickness past unknown,
> His Death was instant, and without a groan.
>
> [ll. 392-403]

In continuing, Pope expresses a desire for just such simplicity, naturalness, and innocence of discord and strife. As indicated by the absence of the sexual language characteristic of earlier sections of the poem, Pope also seems desirous of abandoning the burden and the stress of writing. "Sick of Fops, and Poetry, and Prate, / To *Bufo* [he] left the whole *Castalian* State" (ll. 229-30). When he turns, finally, to his mother, Pope in effect changes places with her, becoming *her* nurse and mother:

> Me, let the tender Office long engage
> To rock the Cradle of reposing Age,
> With lenient Arts extend a Mother's breath,
> Make Languor smile, and smooth the Bed of Death,
> Explore the Thought, explain the asking Eye,
> And keep a while one Parent from the Sky!
>
> [ll. 408-13]

By the end of *Arbuthnot*, certainly, Pope appears different (from "himself"), adopting his father as model and ideal, thus implicitly criticizing his own earlier stance and attitude, and apparently hoping to repeat somehow the innocence the elder Pope represents. But even as he adopts his father as model, Pope—in a different sense—adopts his mother, changing places with her. He thus appears stereotypically "manly" in at best problematical ways.[21] In other words, Pope now deconstructs the earlier account of his manliness, becoming equivocal and womanly. In fact, however, Pope is no different from the way he has always been; he simply makes explicit what was earlier implicit. All along, he has been divided, equivocal. All along, that is, despite his desire to project "manly ways," Pope has not only had feminine ways imposed on him, but he has himself exhibited such ways. For example, in defending his hard-hitting truth-telling ("The truth once told, (and wherefore shou'd we lie?)," l. 81), Pope occasionally resembles a coquette, asking coyly, "You think this cruel?" (l. 83) and "Whom have I hurt?" (l. 95). When he confesses later on, "If wrong, I smil'd; if right, I kiss'd the rod" (l. 158), the *double entendre* indicates the feminine nature of his position. In treating him as a woman, therefore, "the Race that write" were not feminizing Pope. On the contrary, in being split, divided, equivocal, indeterminate, and undecidable, he was already woman.

The term "see-saw" or "oscillation" or perhaps "equivocation" may best describe the relation of male and female in Pope as he appears in *An Epistle to Dr. Arbuthnot*. For there is certainly neither a distinct turn or difference nor a change from one stable and distinct identity into another. Even when supposedly feminine qualities appear most prominently in Pope, at poem's end, they exist alongside—and in oscillation with—"masculine" ones. Thus, even in adopting his peaceable and uncontentious father as model and ideal, Pope continues the (masculine) desire for clear, straight lines and unequivocal truth, the elder

Pope being represented as an absolute. Even if the manifestation changes, the "core" remains, and it is an absolute, unequivocal, and therefore masculine one. That is, the belief in and desire for such definition persists, and of course one desires what one lacks.

The fact is, there are no absolute differences. In spite of what we may think and desire, male and female qualities are coterminous (Chinese philosophy depicts this situation in the yin and the yang, and Galatians 3:28 emphasizes Christ's acceptance and embodiment of this fact: "in Christ there is neither male nor female"). As it happens (and it is finally not surprising), precisely this equivocation, indeterminacy, and undecidability lie at the heart of Pope's most savage satire in *An Epistle to Dr. Arbuthnot,* the scathing portrait of Sporus, traditionally assumed to represent John Lord Hervey, well known for effeminacy of both appearance and manner. But the dramatic and satirical force of the portrait lies not in Sporus's effeminacy but in his combining and embodying "opposite" qualities. According to one of the most illuminating studies of the poem, Sporus is "the very antithesis of the divine reconciliation of opposites."[22] If Atticus is neither quite one thing nor distinctly another, Sporus is, more pointedly and dramatically than Bufo, *both* one thing *and* another, *both* male *and* female: he "Now trips a Lady, and now struts a Lord." "One vile Antithesis. / Amphibious Thing!", Sporus *is* "all see-saw between *that* and *this.*" In Sporus, differences go unreconciled. Whereas in Pope's other treatments differences are finally resolved, synthesized, or somehow transcended, here they stubbornly remain differences, apparently producing emptiness and impotence.

> let me flap this Bug with gilded wings,
> This painted Child of Dirt that stinks and stings;
> Whose Buzz the Witty and the Fair annoys,

Yet Wit ne'er tastes, and Beauty ne'er enjoys,
So well-bred Spaniels civilly delight
In mumbling of the Game they dare not bite.
Eternal Smiles his Emptiness betray,
As shallow streams run dimpling all the way.
Whether in florid Impotence he speaks,
And, as the Prompter breathes, the Puppet squeaks;
Or at the Ear of *Eve*, familiar Toad,
Half Froth, half Venom, spits himself abroad,
In Puns, or Politicks, or Tales, or Lyes,
Or Spite, or Smut, or Rymes, or Blasphemies.
His Wit all see-saw between *that* and *this*,
Now high, now low, now Master up, now Miss,
And he himself one vile Antithesis.
Amphibious Thing! that acting either Part,
The trifling Head, or the corrupted Heart!
Fop at the Toilet, Flatt'rer at the Board,
Now trips a Lady, and now struts a Lord.
Eve's Tempter thus the Rabbins have exprest,
A Cherub's face, a Reptile all the rest;
Beauty that shocks you, Parts that none will trust,
Wit that can creep, and Pride that licks the dust.

[ll. 309-33]

As Aubrey Williams points out, the name "Sporus" de-
rives, at least in part, from the youth that the emperor
Nero had castrated and then, treating him as a woman,
eventually married.[23] Accordingly, Sporus appears in *Ar-
buthnot* as self-divided and different from "himself," ex-
actly like woman as Derrida describes her. Moreover, also
as Derrida suggests, the negative side of the coin that is
Sporus, which represents Pope's declaration of his equiv-
ocation as impotence, is only half the story. For the name
"Sporus" also suggests "spore," which comes from the
Greek word meaning both seed and the act of sowing.
Whereas, then, Sporus as a historical reference suggests
the undecidability and emptiness Pope emphasizes in the

portrait, the etymology of the word denotes—differently—fertility and productivity. Alongside the first, this second, positive meaning is always "present" in the word as a shimmering, or "trace," that prevents the meaning, like the character, from lying still or being unequivocal. This other side of the coin suggests that an internal split, an equivocation, such as Pope (and before him, Hamlet) feared, has positive potential and may be productive.

In any case, the textual situation of indeterminacy between Sporus as potential and as impotent functions as an analogue, as does the "trace" structure of the word "Sporus," of the both/and nature Pope (satirically) ascribes to this figure. The self-division satirized in Sporus is also an analogue of the internal difference within Pope's poem between the various declarations and the descriptions that emerged via our reading. The fissure in *Arbuthnot* marks, of course, the self-difference in Pope, both he and his poem being divided, oscillating, like Sporus, "all see-saw between *that* and *this*." Appearing in each of these situations is a both/and structure, a dividing that is at the same time a joining. If, as a result, identities are nullified, so are absolute differences. Made possible by self-division, indeed impossible without it, is relationality, a point that *The Dunciad* returns to. The structure thus revealed, writes J. Hillis Miller in another but related context, "allows an osmotic mixing, making the stranger friend, the distant near, the *Unheimlich heimlich* . . . without, for all its closeness and similarity, ceasing to be strange, distant, and dissimilar."[24] Self-difference, and equivocation, may not be so bad after all.

If, as Miller claims, an "uncanny antithetical relationship," resulting from inevitable self-difference, "reforms itself in each polar opposite when that opposite is separated out," subverting or nullifying "the apparently unequivocal relation of polarity,"[25] there is, among other things, an obvious and significant effect on Pope's relationship to those he hates and ridicules. Unwilling (lover and) patron, Pope is nevertheless host to the parasite-poetasters in the sense that they "live" inside his poem, taking life from it and being preserved in it. As Pope declares, "Ev'n such small Critics some regard may claim, / Preserv'd in *Milton*'s or in *Shakespear*'s name" (ll. 167-68).[26] At the same time, like Bufo fed by his parasite-hosts, Pope is a parasite as well as a host: he needs the dunces no less than they need him, for without them he would have no poem.

Despite, then, Pope's strong desire for, and determined efforts to achieve, absolute difference, he is only always already *related* to those that he hates and from whom he would distinguish himself. Rather than absolutely *different from* such satirized objects as Bufo and Sporus, he is *like* them, a point long suspected concerning satirists, who, it is often said, fiercely attack in others what they subconsciously realize about themselves. *An Epistle to Dr. Arbuthnot* shows how Pope, in becoming woman, makes clear his own equivocation and indeterminacy, even as he attacks these qualities in those he hates. Thus what he writes in *To a Lady* concerning the contradictory and contrary Atossa both echoes Paul's lament in Romans ("what I hate, that do I," 7:15) and describes "himself":

> Scarce once herself, by turns all Womankind!
> Who, with herself, or others, from her birth
> Finds all her life one warfare upon earth:
> Shines, in exposing Knaves, and painting Fools,
> Yet is, whate'er she hates and ridicules.   [ll. 116-20]

Writing is the name of such *différance*, a point that Pope dramatizes in *Arbuthnot* and acknowledges in *Epistle* I.i.

when he declares that he "grow[s] all to all" (l. 32), being "Careless how ill I with myself agree" (l. 175). That *différance* becomes woman. Writing and woman and Pope: wherein lies the difference./?

⤷ *Chapter Six*

"All Relation Scorn"

Duncery, Deconstruction, and The Dunciad

The Dunciad is clearly Pope's most complex poem, in part because it is more than poem, consisting of poetic text, elaborate notes, and seemingly endless prefatory and other matter. But as Wallace Jackson has recently claimed, "The *New Dunciad* incorporates little that has not been in Pope's texts from the beginning."[1] Focusing on such issues as parts-whole and inside/outside, *The Dunciad* returns us to the concerns with which we began this study. As it reminds us of *An Essay on Criticism* as well as *An Essay on Man,* Pope's last and perhaps greatest poem also extends strategies developed in *Sober Advice from Horace* and covers again some territory explored in *An Epistle to Dr. Arbuthnot,* posing anew questions concerning male and female and self and other. The relation of *The Dunciad* to *Arbuthnot* is, I think, particularly interesting and important, for both poems raise in insistent ways the issue of relationship, most notably via the question of Pope's relations to those he hates and ridicules. Without, I hope, repeating too much of our preceding discussions, I focus here on the relation of Pope, those he attacks, and deconstruction, which seems importantly to resemble duncery as Pope presents it.

A War with Words

In his classic *Pope's "Dunciad": A Study of Its Meaning*, Aubrey Williams argues eloquently that Pope's "war" with duncery is, in the final analysis, "a battle over words— over a destructive use of the 'word,' as the poet saw it, by the dunces in the most important areas of human experience: literature, education, politics, religion."[2] Williams links up *The Dunciad* with the persistent Battle of the Ancients and Moderns:

The War of the Dunces (and that of the Ancients and Moderns) is best described, perhaps, as one waged between eighteenth-century versions of humanist and schoolman. To describe the fray in these terms is to see the parties involved as standing on either side of a cleavage in thought and attitude which extends through the whole of Western civilization: the labels applied to the opposing parties change, but the parties contend about the same issues.[3]

"At the heart of the struggle," in Williams's view, lies "the concern with the means, use, ends, limits of human knowledge," humanists being especially concerned about rhetorical "degeneration into mere words, empty and meaningless verbalism." Their opponents, on the other hand, are of two kinds, but their similarities are stronger than their (superficial) differences: one group reveals logical, dialectical, and scientific preoccupation with things, and the other is concerned with words as outer, material shells at the expense of the informing sense.[4]

Even if the humanists and their opponents do not *always* contend about *exactly* the same issues Williams well describes, we may forever be refighting the Battle of the Ancients and Moderns. In our own day, as Geoffrey Hartman has claimed,[5] that battle is waged between traditional, humanistic critics and "hermeneutical" ones, most notably perhaps deconstructionists. *The Dunciad* may precisely interest many readers today as a prescient treatment of just the issue that Hartman describes. Even if Pope sometimes practices deconstruction, might his hatred and ridicule of Dulness and the dunces be read, then, as another Ancient, humanist attack on the latest version of "Modern madness"?

Duncery and Absence

I am not the first to treat difference (and relation) in *The Dunciad*. Fredric V. Bogel has argued that Pope's last great work "is a poem about relations, especially those relations whose relationship to each other . . . makes meaning possible at all: the relations of sameness and difference."[6] A humanist, Bogel contends that the poet *creates* such relationships, in fact making a difference that did not previously exist. But as I have argued elsewhere,[7] and as Bogel's own text evinces, sameness is not, and cannot be, originary and grounding. If—to take one of Bogel's major points—Dulness is "unrestrained combinatory energy," which unifies "discrete items," difference obviously precedes her efforts to combine.[8] Difference, in fact, already appears (as it must) in the chaos Dulness contemplates at 1.55-78, a passage in which Bogel locates primal undifferentiation: that here "Tragedy and Comedy embrace" (l. 69) and "Farce and Epic get a jumbled race" (l. 70) makes clear that mingling *follows* difference. Ultimately, then, despite its suggestiveness and insight, Bogel's account fails to do justice to the poem because it seems unaware of the work of *différance*.

At issue between us, it might be said, is the difference between *e* and *a*, a difference apparent only in writing. If this is so, if the quarrel concerns words (actually, letters), then we (I!) who engage in the squabble are no different from the dunces, who are satirized for exploiting the very difference I have noted. As one of the more illustrious of them boasts,

> 'Tis true, on Words is still our whole debate,
> Disputes of *Me* or *Te*, of *aut* or *at*,
> To sound or sink in *cano*, O or A,
> Or give up Cicero to C or K.   [4.219-22]

Are we, then, in quarreling with Bogel (and others) implicating ourselves in Pope's capacious satire, *The Dunciad* reading and satirizing us, just as I suggested other Pope poems may do? Does the declaration *"Out of thine own Mouth will I judge thee, wicked Scribler!"* refer as much to us as to the (earlier) dunces?[9] Is deconstruction (merely) a war with words? Such questions bear on the poem's remarkable capacity for drawing seemingly everything into its own vortex, not unlike Dulness herself sucking all in.

Let us continue for a while to look at the dunces' war with words. What "Bentley," the "verbal Critick," favors in the passage above (as well as in the notes to *Sober Advice*) is also what the Goddess promotes. Nothing would advance her cause more, the poem maintains, than general *verbal* warfare; she wants human concern narrowed to a "war with Words alone" (4.178). That is precisely what is being taught in the schools, already victims of her sway. That duncery permeates the educational establishment is not surprising, Pope declares, since Dulness is "often rec-

onciled in some degree with Learning" (4.21-22n.). Ex-
emplifying the current teaching, Dr. Busby, the famous
headmaster of Westminster, asserts:

> "Since Man from beast by Words is known,
> Words are Man's province, Words we teach alone.
> When Reason doubtful, like the Samian letter,
> Points him two ways, the narrower is the better.
> Plac'd at the door of Learning, youth to guide,
> We never suffer it to stand too wide.
> To ask, to guess, to know, as they commence,
> As Fancy opens the quick springs of Sense,
> We ply the Memory, we load the brain,
> Bind rebel Wit, and double chain on chain,
> Confine the thought, to exercise the breath;
> And keep them in the pale of Words till death.
> [4.149-60]

What Pope specifically opposes in Dulness's call to "war
with Words alone," in Busby's proclamation that "words"
the schools "teach alone," and in Bentley's boast that "on
Words is still our whole debate" is what he evidently
feared in *An Essay on Criticism* and attacked in both the
verse and the notes of *Sober Advice from Horace*: a privi-
leging of the shell at the expense of the heart and soul of
the matter. For Pope, "sense *informs* words,"[10] just as "In
some fair Body . . . th' informing Soul / With Spirits feeds,
with Vigour fills the whole, / . . . / *It self unseen*, but in th'
Effects, remains" (*An Essay on Criticism*, ll. 76-79); for the
dunces, however, words are *merely* material things. The
notes to *The Dunciad*, often parodying Richard Bentley
and exposing his pedantry as well as that of Scriblerus and
others, dramatize the dunces' abusive neglect of inform-
ing sense.

Pope's treatment, in the verse, of the antiquarian coin
collectors Annius and Mummius (4.347-94) and of the

gardener and the naturalist (4.397-436) plays a variation on the same theme. The antiquarians are concerned with coins as material things, Annius ironically dramatizing the primacy (for Pope) of the informing sense when he ingests the coins he has stolen. Meddling "only in [his own] sphere" (l. 432), the naturalist destroys—it seems—anything that gets in the way of his "insect lust" (l. 415): as he insensitively replies to the gardener's anguished cry, wherever the prized butterfly "fix'd, the beauteous bird I seiz'd: / Rose or Carnation was below my care" (ll. 430-31). Of course, the distraught gardener is no less a (narrow) specialist and no less willing, in Aubrey Williams's apt phrasing, to "focus extravagantly upon nature itself and grant to the thing the devotion properly given to God."[11] For their contributions, in helping "T'invert the world, and counter-work its Cause" (*An Essay on Man* 3.244) and thus to "MAKE ONE MIGHTY DUNCIAD OF THE LAND" (4.604), the antiquarians, the gardener, and the scientist receive Dulness's commendation. They have helped to narrow men's outlook and to make them forget about God:

> "O! would the Sons of Men once think their Eyes
> And Reason giv'n them but to study *Flies!*
> See Nature in some partial narrow shape,
> And let the Author of the Whole escape:
> Learn but to trifle; or, who most observe,
> To wonder at their Maker, not to serve."   [ll. 453-58]

According to Pope, those who valorize natural and material objects produce the same effects as those who restrict their concern to words alone.

Scientist and scholar alike, Pope maintains, neglect what is central to any intellectual effort, and that is *use*, a point that recalls Pope's focus on "the use of riches" in the

Moral Essays. As Bentley puts it, echoing Dulness's prayer just quoted:

> The critic Eye, that microscope of Wit,
> Sees hairs and pores, examines bit by bit:
> How parts relate to parts, or they to whole,
> The body's harmony, the beaming soul,
> Are things which Kuster, Burman, Wasse shall see,
> When Man's whole frame is obvious to a *Flea.*
>
> [ll. 233-38]

This "verbal Critick" adds, "we dim the eyes, and stuff the head / With all such reading as was never read" (ll. 249-50), helping to produce pedants like himself rather than citizen-humanists, the ideal of the tradition out of which Pope writes. Bentley's conclusion is, "We only furnish what [you] cannot use" (l. 261). For Pope, on the other hand, what mattered was wisdom, and wisdom derives, as Williams puts it, from "the whole man as a single moral, religious, and sentient being"; it also involves "the *use* of learning for the benefit of others."[12]

Pope's particular depiction of duncery as neglectful of informing sense carries still further implications, as Williams has shown. It is, he writes, "impossible to separate the war 'over words' which gave the poem its impetus, and the theological metaphor which gives it its profoundest significance."[13] Though Williams's interpretation has recently been challenged, the theological implications of Pope's efforts seem to me obvious.[14] To begin with, *The Dunciad* clearly inverts *An Essay on Man*, its plea for charity and relationality, and its call to move outward, from the self, toward others, in love. Instead of expanding love, movingly described at the end of *An Essay on Man, The Dunciad* offers Dulness's inwardly spiraling vortex, ever-narrowing concern (the goal is "A trifling head, and a contracted heart," 4.504), a god "Wrapt up in Self" (4.485), and the injunction to "all Relation scorn, / See all in *Self*, and but for self be born" (4.479-80).

Inversion thus plays a major role in the later poem. According to Williams, "as Pope employs this principle of inversion in the *Dunciad* it is more than a matter of technique: it is also a realization of the nature of evil, of its negative and destructive qualities." In Christian thought, as Williams says, evil is "neither 'an essence nor a nature nor a form' but an absence, a privation, a non-being."[15] Such emptiness and absence characterize the dunces' understanding of the "word," as well as the soulless metaphysics of Dulness. According to Bentley, emphasizing duncery's devotion to surfaces and exteriors:

> Like buoys, that never sink into the flood,
> On Learning's surface we but lie and nod.
> Thine is the genuine head of many a house,
> And much Divinity without a *Noῦς*.   [4.241-44]

As Pope carefully explains in a note to this last line, *Noῦς* is a "word much affected by the learned Aristarchus in common conversation, to signify *Genius* or natural *acumen*. But this passage has a farther view," he continues, for "*Noῦς* was the Platonic term for *Mind*, or the *first Cause*, and that system of Divinity is here hinted at which terminates in blind Nature without a *Noῦς*." Content to "See Nature in some partial narrow shape, / And let the Author of the Whole escape" (4.455-56), that way of thinking comes to rest in secondariness, with things, not being "to Nature's Cause thro' Nature led" (4.468). Such "free-thinkers," as Pope calls them in the note to line 501,

> Make Nature still incroach upon [God's] plan;
> And shove him off as far as e'er we can:

Thrust some Mechanic Cause into his place;
Or bind in Matter, or diffuse in Space.
Or, at one bound o'er-leaping all his laws,
Make God Man's Image, Man the final Cause.

[4.473-78]

Words and world alike are emptied of meaning, leaving a shell, and the absence, the non-being, made "present" in *The Dunciad* is figured by Pope as evil.

Duncery and Deconstruction

What we have seen about Dulness and duncery suggests a link with deconstruction. A (castrated and castrating) *woman*, opposing the male *Logos* and menacing the regnant logo- and phallogocentrism; an *inversion* of humanistic understanding and values; a representation of *absence*; an advocate of the study of *words* alone, their sounds, and their materiality; a champion of *exteriors* and *surfaces*; a skeptic concerning a *"final Cause"* and a promoter of secondariness—are not these and other characteristics of Dulness shared by deconstruction? Is deconstruction, which becomes woman, one of Pope's satirical objects in *The Dunciad?* To raise such a question seems to participate in duncery's work of inversion.

Of course, it is not just in the characterization of Dulness that *The Dunciad* parallels (aspects of) deconstruction, its teaching, and its effects. Considered as poem and commentary, *The Dunciad*, with its voluminous notes and elaborate editorial apparatus, is part of an entire tradition, in which deconstruction participates and which is concerned to explore such questions as the relation between "text" and commentary. One thinks immediately of *A Tale of a Tub, Sartor Resartus,* and *Pale Fire* as well as of such decentering efforts by Derrida as *Glas* and "Living On: Border Lines." By means of typographical strategies, Derrida succeeds in problematizing our usual notions concerning margins, borders, and the "proper," "Living On" consisting of an essay placed as a footnote that contends for priority with the essay "proper." In *The Dunciad,* the notes, and less frequently the prefatory and other matter, serve a number of purposes. The notes are of several kinds, some continuing and extending the satire at work in the verse, others exposing the wrongheadedness of Scriblerus, Bentley, Cibber, Theobald, et al. The effect of many of these notes is simply to present the work of "verbal Criticks." This work the Goddess describes as follows:

> ". . . murder first, and mince them all to bits;
> As erst Medea (cruel, so to save!)
> A new Edition of old Æson gave,
> Let standard-Authors, thus, like trophies born,
> Appear more glorious as more hack'd and torn,
> And you, my Critics! in the chequer'd shade,
> Admire new light thro' holes yourselves have made.
> "Leave not a foot of verse, a foot of stone,
> A Page, a Grave, that they can call their own;
> But spread, my sons, your glory thin or thick,
> On passive paper, or on solid brick.   [4.120-30]

Though most of the notes serve some satirical purpose, still others provide helpful—and in some cases, essential—information and clarification. Regardless of their nature, the overall effect of the panoply of notes is, as William Kinsley has written, to "crowd the poem off the page," much as the "prefaces and appendices reproduce their kind to the seventh generation."[16] Like Swift in *A Tale of a Tub,* which ironically mingles "text" and commentary, Pope wants things straight, center and margins clearly distinct, and so the extensive editorial apparatus is designed to satirize the indulgent dunces, who—we might say—have become de-centered (though not morally). On this matter of textual boundaries, Kinsley further writes that "one of the most important benefits of printing for [Pope] was its rigid spatial separation of text and commentary. . . . [M]arginal glosses, the manuscript equivalent of footnotes, always had a fateful tendency to creep into the text and lodge there. Once the spatial separation is firmly established, Pope is free to set up many kinds of ironical relationships between text and commentary."[17]

Actually, the relationship between "text" and commentary is no more stable in *The Dunciad* than in the manuscripts that Kinsley mentions: the "rigid spatial separation" does not tell the whole story. I have already suggested the point in claiming that some of the notes continue and expand the satire and that still others provide needed information. Aubrey Williams made this last point some time ago, though without drawing the significance that I am interested in. He wrote, in discussing how many of the notes serve as justification for Pope's attacks in the verse, that "the notes . . . are an implicit admission of a kind of failure, but they are also an attempt to remedy the situation, particularly with regard to the ethical vision of the poet. Because the notes are not the poem, however, even the remedy is not ultimately a thoroughly satisfactory solution to the problem: the damage is in some ways skilfully repaired, but one can still see the patches."[18] *The Dunciad* qua poem is not, then, a whole—only holey. The notes *supplement*, trying to plug some of these holes. As they supplement the flawed "text," the notes break down any "rigid" separation between "text" and notes. What is ostensibly a satirical technique turns out to be more: Pope's own text displays the same de-centering for which he satirizes the dunces.

A final point or two concerning the notes, which in various ways call in question the notion of the "proper": They not only supplement the verse, but they also act to open up the text, destabilizing it and exposing it as something other than—because more than—a fixed and complete object, a well-wrought urn. In short, the notes establish the text's need for help, from readers. As Williams writes, the notes impose "upon editors and critics a never-ending (though in part fruitless) job of clarification, a laborious correction of Pope's careful misstatements of fact."[19] Several of the (in more than one sense, modern) notes in the Twickenham Edition mirror the dunces' editorial labors, annotating *their* commentary, trying to set matters straight, providing factual information, and explaining certain apparently obscure allusions.[20] If, as Kinsley claims, "Pope implies that the *Dunciad* . . . can assimilate all future commentary into itself,"[21] it also makes clear its receptivity to such commentary, extending an invitation to annotate and supplement. To whom, then, does the text "properly" belong?

Of course, *The Dunciad* opens up in another way, a way to which the notes themselves do not contribute significantly. The poem is not complete "in itself" because it is involved with, parallels, and extends such other poems as *An Essay on Man.* More so than any other of Pope's major poems, *The Dunciad* reveals the ways in which texts interpenetrate each other. As I suggested earlier, it is importantly related, not only to *An Essay on Man,* but also to *An Essay on Criticism, Sober Advice from Horace,* and *An Epistle to Dr. Arbuthnot,* as well as (obviously) to the three-book *Dunciad* of the late 1720s. In being involved with such texts, *The Dunciad* spills over, exceeding "itself" as a self-contained entity.

I want to mention one other way in which the poem prevents us from rounding it off. To indicate how it opens "itself" up still further, I turn to the recent argument by Donald T. Siebert, Jr., that critics such as Aubrey Williams have painted too pessimistic a picture of what *The Dunciad* is. It may be, as Siebert claims, that "the School of Deep Intent" slights and on occasion ignores the wit and humor that permeate the poem, though I do not see how one can discount the philosophical and theological meanings that Williams describes. The situation, I think, resembles that in *Sober Advice from Horace*: Pope *is* serious, deeply so, about the threat posed by the dunces. At the same time, there is the smut and the fun especially of the first three books, and we enjoy and delight in it, as Pope must have. Surely part—and not a negligible part, at that—of the meaning and significance of *The Dunciad* lies in the game and the play, including the often brilliant fiction of the seemingly endless commentary.[22] And as Geoffrey Hartman has observed, there are carnivalesque qualities aplenty in Pope and an "older, hieratic speech, biblical, mystical, or popular-sermonic, [that] pierces with 'Asiatic' force through 'Attic' veils."[23] Perhaps contrary to the implications of "the School of Deep Intent," the smutty fun is not transcended (or not fully so, anyway), and, perhaps contrary to Siebert's argument, that fun does not obscure the seriousness. I am not suggesting that in *The Dunciad* the fun and the "deep Intent" (4.4) always work together or co-exist harmoniously. On the contrary, they seem to reside together in uneasy tension that is never quite resolved—a situation paralleled, as we shall see, by other features. Thanks to the dialogical nature of satire, Pope can put the earthy counterheroic rhetoric in the mouths of the dunces, thereby indulging in it while condemning it. But the play, like other features, spills over, affecting the "deep Intent," helping to make the poem exceed "itself," just as *An Essay on Criticism* exceeds "itself."

The Dunciad contains, then, features and effects that cannot always (to echo Barbara Johnson) be reasonably attributed to Pope's conscious intentions.

Defeating One's Own Design

In *The Dunciad*, Pope's basic technique consists of letting the "wicked scriblers" condemn themselves out of their own mouths, turning their own words against them. As a result, "In broad Effulgence all below [is] reveal'd" (4.18). As he does elsewhere, then, Pope here reads against the grain, the duces exposing themselves in spite of themselves.

Despite obvious differences, accentuated by Pope's desire to appear and be different from the duces, he is in some ways like them, his actions on occasion mirroring theirs. Consider, for example, what Aubrey Williams calls Pope's "careful misstatements of fact" in the notes, where he plays fast and loose with the texts of duncery so as to implicate and convict the votaries of Dulness. Not content to let the duces be judged by their own words, even if one reads those words counter to their authors' intentions, Pope sometimes puts into their mouths something other than what they actually wrote or were known to have said. Such fabrications are not so different from the counterfeiting done, for example, by the London booksellers whom Pope castigates. Such counterfeiting Dulness applauds, as she makes clear in speaking to Curll, an expert at this work:

> "Son! thy grief lay down,
> And turn this whole illusion on the town:
> As the sage dame, experienc'd in her trade,
> By names of Toasts retails each batter'd jade;

(Whence hapless Monsieur much complains at Paris
Of wrongs from Duchesses and Lady Maries;)
Be thine, my stationer! this magic gift;
Cook shall be Prior, and Concanen, Swift:
So shall each hostile name become our own,
And we too boast our Garth and Addison."

[2.131-40]

I do not deny the differences, including those in the eyes
of the law, between the fraudulent bookseller and the sa-
tirical poet. I do, though, insist on the structural similarity
in their actions, both counterfeiting: albeit in different
ways, Curll and Pope make "each hostile name . . . [their]
own."[24]

That Pope resembles such dunces as his archenemy Ed-
mund Curll more closely than he would care to admit,
appears too in the manner in which he depicts himself in
the final book. As the opening verses suggest ("Yet, yet a
moment, one dim Ray of Light / Indulge, dread Chaos,
and eternal Night!"), Pope sets out to dramatize the power
and effects of Dulness, evincing that even he, poet of light
and Being and defender of distinction and difference,
must succumb as "the all-composing Hour / Resistless
falls" (ll. 627-28); the schools, the church, the arts, and
government have already enlisted in her efforts to extin-
guish all light. Though he by no means becomes a votary
of the Goddess, Pope feels her "resistless" sway to such a
degree that Scriblerus mistakes him for one of her party,
referring to him not only as "a dull Poet" (l. 4n.) but also
as her "genuine Son" (l. 1n.). Any other strategy would
have endangered Pope's efforts: had such a person as Pope
remained untouched by Dulness's effects, readers would
not have been so disturbed by the dire prospects. But Pope
obviously wanted his readers to appreciate the gravity of
the threat as he perceived it—and as he powerfully de-
scribes it toward the close of the poem.

In a note at the end of Book III "signed" by Scriblerus, Pope warns his readers not to mistake the power and influence of Dulness but to recognize them as the threat they are. This note immediately precedes, and prepares the way for, the dramatized effects of Dulness's sway on the poet in the final book. "It may perhaps seem incredible, that so great a Revolution in Learning as is here prophesied, should be brought about by such *weak Instruments* as have been described in our poem: But do not thou, gentle reader, rest too secure in thy contempt of these Instruments" (l. 333n.).

In Book IV, Pope contradicts this statement, reassuring us that, no matter how threatening duncery may appear, it will subvert its own efforts, and so there is nothing to worry about: ". . . if it be well consider'd, . . . whatever inclination they might have to do mischief, her sons are generally render'd harmless by their Inability; and . . . it is the common effect of Dulness (even in her greatest efforts) to defeat her own design" (4.584n.). Pope's contradiction might be dismissed as an unimportant slip, to which we are all prone, were it not that this particular contradiction mirrors exactly the subversion said to be characteristic of Dulness and the dunces. In undermining in the fourth book of *The Dunciad* the claim made in the third, Pope reveals another similarity to Dulness: like her, he defeats his own design.

Accepting Relation

The question of Pope's relation to those he hates and ridicules opens out onto the larger matter of relation in general, a topic that *The Dunciad* thematizes. An issue important in Pope's poetry since *An Essay on Criticism*, it appears most prominently here in the speech of the

"gloomy Clerk." Having boasted that, a "Sworn foe to
Myst'ry" (4.460), he like the other dunces will not be "to
Nature's Cause thro' Nature led" (l. 468), the clergyman
declares:

> All-seeing in thy mists, we want no guide,
> Mother of Arrogance, and Source of Pride!
> We nobly take the high Priori Road,
> And reason downward, till we doubt of God:
> Make Nature still incroach upon his plan;
> And shove him off as far as e'er we can:
> Thrust some Mechanic Cause into his place;
> Or bind in Matter, or diffuse in Space.
> Or, at one bound o'er-leaping all his laws,
> Make God Man's Image, Man the final Cause,
> Find Virtue local, all Relation scorn,
> See all in *Self*, and but for self be born:
> Of nought so certain as our *Reason* still,
> Of nought so doubtful as of *Soul* and *Will*.
> Oh hide the God still more! and make us see
> Such as Lucretius drew, a God like Thee:
> Wrapt up in Self, a God without a Thought,
> Regardless of our merit or default.   [ll. 469-86]

No more devastating self-exposure occurs in *The Dunciad*
as inversions of traditional understanding abound: taking
the place of the grand conception of Nature, extolled in
An Essay on Criticism and *An Essay on Man*, which bodies
forth God's design, is a mechanical, soulless, and materi-
alistic notion, and man has usurped the power and place
of God, accomplishing what Pope's theodicy satirized him
for daring. If God exists at all, the Clerk shamelessly
maintains, He is "without a Thought," "a Divinity without
a Νοῦς."

The inversions in this and other passages, it is impor-
tant to understand, are part of Pope's "thoroughgoing

technique."[25] Accustomed as many (most?) are to think of literary texts as simply mimetic, we may find it hard to grasp that inversion in *The Dunciad* is not primarily what duncery effects but, rather, a device that Pope employs to represent the activity of Dulness and her followers. I want to consider some of the implications of using inversion to represent threats to one's cherished beliefs.

To begin with, if everything is inverted, man, for example, becoming the Final Cause, hierarchization is (obviously) preserved, an either/or situation prevailing: either God or man assumes priority. In light of Pope's defense of the *Logos,* such a situation is hardly surprising. Hierarchies are, of course, maintained by violence, and inverting is oppositional (and therefore violent) as well as hierarchical. But if inversion is oppositional, it contradicts Pope's call to relation. As he did in *An Essay on Man,* Pope denies, in 4.469-86, that virtue is "local," pertaining only to an isolated "part" or "parts" unconcerned with how such a "part" relates to another. But the dunces, Pope claims, "all Relation scorn"; for them what matters is the operation of the individual "part," in isolation. Such a belief ultimately ends, Pope maintains, with each "center[ing] every thing in *himself*" (l. 478n.). But isn't the belief that Pope ascribes to the dunces, denying that virtue is relational, the logical conclusion of the logocentrism that Pope defends? Rigid separation, absolute difference, distinct identity—these preclude relation.

The relationship that Pope seeks thus does not reside comfortably with the logocentrism that characterizes his efforts to achieve it. Indeed, those procedures ensure that relationality will not result. Committed equally to opposing, Pope can only invert, making what he hates and fears the *opposite* of what he cherishes, as he did in *An Epistle to Dr. Arbuthnot.* Caught in the trap of binary oppositions, fundamental to logocentrism, Pope denies himself what he seeks. Inverting, Pope understands Dulness and the dunces as merely destructive, indeed as (maternal) absence and non-being, and so he opposes to them (paternal) presence and Being. Another procedure, eschewing oppositionalism and inversion, would lead to a sense of relatedness to those from whom Pope wants to difference himself absolutely. But as we saw in *Arbuthnot,* as well as in *The Dunciad,* such relations always already exist; in a number of ways, Pope is like those he hates and ridicules, resembling his "opponents" in spite of himself.

Preceding man, relation is not dependent on him for its "existence" and effects. It plays and does its work in spite of him, undermining his oppositional ways. The key to relationality appears to lie in the fact of self-difference, which itself derives from what Derrida terms (in a passage I quoted in the first chapter) the "trace retaining the other as other in the same." Considering differences between divinity and humanity in light of the "trace," John Dominic Crossan has made precisely this point. We may substitute any other "opposition," for example self and other, for those Crossan deconstructs: "If humanity and divinity must be separated, they are combined by that very disjunction itself; and if humanity and divinity are to be joined, they are separated as well by that necessity. Whether a hybrid is to be censored or celebrated, the difference that establishes it, be it for separation or for combination, rules alike over both those options and is much more fundamental than either of them. The difference is itself a relationship that binds more firmly than any other could."[26] As Crossan stipulates, "*it makes a difference*" whether you privilege divinity or humanity, just as it does whether you are (or embrace) Pope or the dunces. Still, as Derrida insists, *différance* is "the movement that structures every dissociation."[27]

I perhaps cannot stress enough that difference operates

within entities as well as between them, and it is their self-difference, *différance*, the retention of a "trace" of the "other" as other in the "same," that produces relation. For Herbert N. Schneidau, whom I mentioned earlier in this book, that self-difference is a mode of alienation, and achieving some alienation from ourselves, he maintains, is very good news indeed.[28] Crucial, it seems, is somehow coming to realize our internal division, accepting it, and regarding it as a way of getting outside the self considered as a fragile, precious, univocal bearer of meaning and significance. To transcend the self and its proud, vain desires and imposed meanings, reaching a point where we can be critical of them, requires recognizing and admitting the presence of an *other*, the "trace" in us of an other, which is always already a part of us.

In *The Dunciad*, Pope declares the need for just such an other:

> Kind Self-conceit to some her glass applies,
> Which no one looks in with another's eyes:
> But as the Flatt'rer or Dependant paint,
> Beholds himself a Patriot, Chief, or Saint.   [4.533-36]

One is, then, not enough. Pope "himself," as we have seen, contains the needed *other* within himself, a point that Bogel approaches in treating, in a footnote, Pope's "closing appeal to the Muse": "O sing, and hush the Nations with thy Song!" (4.626). According to Bogel, the line shows the speaker turning "rather dramatically into his opposite," the word "hush"—"a *lapsus linguae*"—marking "an invasion of the self by the other or a recognition that what had been conceived of as other is actually present in the self."[29] But the situation is not quite as Bogel describes it. The latter half of the coordinate construction in the immediately preceding quotation accurately describes the relation of self and other, though Bogel presents it as equivalent to the very different position indicated in the former half. Clearly, the other does not invade the self from outside. Rather, it is always already *in* the self, self and other being related, neither being conceivable or having any meaning apart from the other.

"Always a case of both/and, never a simple either/or"

If—to return to my earlier contention—Dulness parallels deconstruction in inverting traditional, humanistic understanding, that resemblance ends if her work stops with inversion. Pope sees and depicts her work as simply that, just as he sees the oscillating, self-divided Sporus as merely negative. Thus duncery relates to deconstruction as a caricature of it, not a faithful representation (deconstruction is not, for example, in any simple sense a war with words alone). In opposing and inverting, Pope ensures that he not be able to recognize that the "other" is a part of him as he is a part of the "other." The implications of such a relationship of "self" and "other" are far-reaching—and obviously bear on religion as well as ethics.[30] Has this study turned out, after all, to be about humanity and divinity and so to be—in some ways—the study of Pope and religion that I had long planned? A trace remains . . .

Notes

Chapter One

1. G. Douglas Atkins, "Pope and Deism: A New Analysis," *Huntington Library Quarterly*, 35 (1972), 257-78; rpt. in *Pope: Recent Essays by Several Hands*, ed. Maynard Mack and James A. Winn (Hamden, Conn.: Archon, 1980), pp. 392-415, 823-28.

2. G. Douglas Atkins, "The Money of Stories of Money," forthcoming in *The Eighteenth Century: Theory and Interpretation.* See also my "'Count It All Joy': The Affirmative Nature of Deconstruction," *University of Hartford Studies in Literature*, 16 (1984), 120-28.

3. Paul de Man, *Allegories of Reading: Figural Language in Rousseau, Nietzsche, Rilke, and Proust* (New Haven: Yale Univ. Press, 1979), p. ix.

4. Jacques Derrida, *Of Grammatology*, trans. Gayatri Chakravorty Spivak (Baltimore: Johns Hopkins Univ. Press, 1976), pp. 14, 13.

5. Paul de Man, Foreword to Carol Jacobs, *The Dissimulating Harmony: The Image of Interpretation in Nietzsche, Rilke, Artaud, and Benjamin* (Baltimore: Johns Hopkins Univ. Press, 1978), pp. ix-x.

6. Ibid., p. xi.

7. G. Douglas Atkins, *Reading Deconstruction / Deconstruc-*

tive Reading (1983; rpt. Lexington: Univ. Press of Kentucky, 1985).

8. Ibid., esp. pp. 49-63, 136-39. I first used the term in discussing the criticism of Geoffrey Hartman, some of whose ideas I incorporate here. See also my essay "Pope's Poetry and the Reader's Responsibility," *College Literature*, 9 (1982), 83-96.

9. Derrida, *Of Grammatology*, p. 158.

10. Geoffrey H. Hartman, *Saving the Text: Literature / Derrida / Philosophy* (Baltimore: Johns Hopkins Univ. Press, 1981), p. 60.

11. Derrida, *Of Grammatology*, p. 158.

12. Jacques Derrida, *Margins of Philosophy*, trans. Alan Bass (Chicago: Univ. of Chicago Press, 1982), p. 326.

13. Derrida, *Of Grammatology*, p. 158.

14. But see *Positions*, trans. Alan Bass (Chicago: Univ. of Chicago Press, 1981), pp. 41-42, where Derrida notes that "the word *phase* is perhaps not the most rigorous one. It is not a question of a chronological phase, a given moment, or a page that one day simply will be turned, in order to go on to other things. The necessity of this phase is structural."

15. Ferdinand de Saussure, *Course in General Linguistics*, trans. Wade Baskin (New York: McGraw-Hill, 1959), p. 67.

16. Derrida, *Positions*, p. 27.

17. Jacques Derrida, "Differance," in *Speech and Phenomena and Other Essays on Husserl's Theory of Signs*, trans. David B. Allison (Evanston: Northwestern Univ. Press, 1973), p. 142.

18. Derrida, *Of Grammatology*, p. 62.

19. Ibid., pp. 144-45.

20. "Translator's Introduction" to Jacques Derrida, *Dissemination*, trans. Barbara Johnson (Chicago: Univ. of Chicago Press, 1981), p. xiii.

21. Ibid., p. xiii.

22. Robert Magliola, *Derrida on the Mend* (West Lafayette, Ind.: Purdue Univ. Press, 1984), pp. 176-77.

23. I too have found examples of Miller's succumbing to binary oppositions; see my "The Story of Error," in *Reading Deconstruction / Deconstructive Reading*, pp. 79-88.

24. Roland Barthes, *S / Z*, trans. Richard Miller (New York: Hill and Wang, 1974), p. 4.

25. See my *Reading Deconstruction / Deconstructive Reading*, esp. pp. 87-88, and Jonathan Culler, *On Deconstruction: Theory and Criticism after Structuralism* (Ithaca: Cornell Univ. Press, 1982), esp. pp. 64-83.

26. Frederick M. Keener, *An Essay on Pope* (New York: Columbia Univ. Press, 1974), p. 5. The Kenner quotation is from "In the Wake of the Anarch," in *Gnomon: Essays on Contemporary Literature* (New York: McDowell, Obolensky, 1958), p. 176. Keener is citing Earl Wasserman on Pope's "ideal contemporary"; see *Pope's "Epistle to Bathurst": A Critical Reading with an Edition of the Manuscripts* (Baltimore: Johns Hopkins Univ. Press, 1960), pp. 14-16.

27. Geoffrey H. Hartman, *Criticism in the Wilderness: The Study of Literature Today* (New Haven: Yale Univ. Press, 1980), pp. 170, 177.

28. Deconstruction also allows us to treat other issues, such as the role of unconscious motives, the neglect of which in Pope criticism George S. Rousseau has recently lamented. See "Writings on the Margins of Pope," *Eighteenth-Century Studies*, 14 (1980-81), 181-93. Rousseau writes, with specific reference to Dustin H. Griffin's *Alexander Pope: The Poet in the Poems*, that "the probable reason for omitting the unconscious motives is not, of course, that Pope did not verbalize them, but rather a result of American graduate-school training. Until recently and in most quarters, psychoanalysis and literary criticism has been frowned upon; a book restricted to conscious concerns, those the poet verbalized—so the argument goes—is capable of containment; it can readily prove its point; it is gentlemanly; it will please the elder statesmen who often disapprove of psychological interpretations. These 'elder statesmen' also decide if a book gets published. I do not dare suggest that the politics of consideration is the sole reason for Griffin's confinement, but no profound insight is required to understand the predilection for conscious over unconscious motives. . . . Such guardedness is one reason that traditional American literary criticism—of which Griffin's book is a fine example—has found itself in decline. It may now be among the least ambitious of all the humanistic disciplines, yet it parades and flaunts its own indifference. No one sensible would want to argue that Pope's reputation, which

is not so high now as some may think, would be greater if radical Popean criticism were in vogue. A Marxist or Freudian reading of Pope is not going to save Pope or popularize him among the masses. But I think it to be self-evident that if Pope's poetry and career had been courageously approached and less restricted to 'conscious domains'—to realms that are safe insofar as they are capable of *proof*—we (the eighteenth-century world) might have claimed more devotees than we now do, and those habitués we captured might think of Pope a bit less than they do as the 'poet of reason' and a bit more as the 'voice of unreason,' and as a creature of flesh and blood" (p. 189). Though I do not share all of Rousseau's concerns, I offer these essays as one response to them.

29. Friedrich Nietzsche, *The Birth of Tragedy*, trans. Walter Kaufmann (New York: Vintage, 1967), p. 95.

30. J. Hillis Miller, "Tradition and Difference," *Diacritics*, 2 (Winter 1972), 13, 12, 13. The Nietzsche quotations are from *The Will to Power*, ed. Walter Kaufmann, trans. Walter Kaufmann and R.J. Hollingdale (New York: Vintage, 1958), pp. 298, 270.

31. For an interesting account of Pope, one that treats difference and relation but is grounded in belief in identity, see Fredric V. Bogel, "Dulness Unbound: Rhetoric and Pope's *Dunciad*," *PMLA*, 97 (1982), 844-55. See also my response, "Pope and Difference," *PMLA*, 98 (1983), 407-8. I discuss Bogel's position in Chapter Six below.

Chapter Two

1. David B. Morris, *Alexander Pope: The Genius of Sense* (Cambridge: Harvard Univ. Press, 1984).

2. I have elsewhere discussed the prominence of this problem in the *Essay*, especially the way it structures the second section; see "Poetic Strategies in *An Essay on Criticism*, Lines 201-559," *South Atlantic Bulletin*, 44 (1979), 43-47.

3. Morris, *Alexander Pope*, p. 67.

4. Ibid., p. 68.

5. Ibid., p. 69. The quotation is from Wentworth Dillon, Earl of Roscommon, *An Essay on Translated Verse* (1684).

6. See the Hack's advice that "whatever reader desires to have a thorough comprehension of an author's thoughts, cannot take a better method, than by putting himself into the circumstances and postures of life, that the writer was in upon every important passage as it flowed from his pen, for this will introduce a parity and strict correspondence of ideas between the reader and the author" (Jonathan Swift, *"Gulliver's Travels" and Other Writings*, ed. Louis A. Landa [Boston: Houghton Mifflin, 1960], p. 265).

7. See Lanham's recent books *The Motives of Eloquence: Literary Rhetoric in the Renaissance* (New Haven: Yale Univ. Press, 1976) and *Literacy and the Survival of Humanism* (New Haven: Yale Univ. Press, 1983). I do not mean to imply that Lanham is a deconstructionist, only that he and the rhetorical tradition he defines have affinities with deconstruction. Viewed in the light of Lanham's discussions, the refusal to rest satisfied with purposiveness alone is simply characteristic of the "rhetorical ideal."

8. Aubrey Williams, ed., *Pastoral Poetry and "An Essay on Criticism,"* the first volume of the Twickenham Edition of the *Poems* (New Haven: Yale Univ. Press, 1961), pp. 212, 209.

9. Aubrey Williams, *Pope's "Dunciad": A Study of Its Meaning* (1955; n.p.: Archon, 1968), pp. 114-15. This classic study provides a valuable account of background pertinent to the *Essay* as well as to Pope's last major poem.

10. Ibid., p. 115.

11. Williams, ed., *Pastoral Poetry and "An Essay on Criticism,"* p. 217.

12. Ibid.

13. Williams, *Pope's "Dunciad,"* p. 112.

14. Thomas Sheridan, *British Education* (London, 1769), pp. 107, 217, 220; quoted in Williams, *Pope's "Dunciad,"* pp. 113-14.

15. Williams, *Pope's "Dunciad,"* p. 112.

16. *Essays of John Dryden*, ed. W.P. Ker (Oxford: Clarendon Press, 1926), I, 193.

17. Cf. Wendy Steiner, *The Colors of Rhetoric: Problems in the Relation between Modern Literature and Painting* (Chicago: Univ. of Chicago Press, 1982).

18. *The Correspondence of Alexander Pope,* ed. George Sherburn (Oxford: Clarendon Press, 1956), II, 378.

19. Williams, *Pope's "Dunciad,"* p. 112.

20. For Derrida on "expression," see, for example, *Positions,* pp. 31-33 and 45, and *Margins of Philosophy,* esp. pp. 157-73.

21. de Man, Foreword to Jacobs, *Dissimulating Harmony,* esp. pp. ix-x.

22. Swift, *"Gulliver's Travels" and Other Writings,* pp. 324-25.

23. Derrida, *Positions,* p. 41.

24. Cleanth Brooks, *The Well-Wrought Urn: Studies in the Structure of Poetry* (New York: Harcourt, Brace, 1947), p. 17.

25. Jonathan Culler, *On Deconstruction: Theory and Criticism after Structuralism* (Ithaca: Cornell Univ. Press, 1982), pp. 138-39. I am indebted, in the next few pages, to Culler's always illuminating discussions.

26. Ibid., p. 204.

27. Ibid., p. 205.

28. Ibid.

29. Jacques Derrida, "Living On: Border Lines," in Harold Bloom et al., *Deconstruction and Criticism* (New York: Seabury, 1979), p. 97.

30. Ibid., p. 98.

31. This is the title of a section of the text *Of Grammatology,* pp. 44-65. Derrida both uses and crosses out the copula. See also Derrida's "The Supplement of Copula: Philosophy *before* Linguistics," in *Textual Strategies: Perspectives in Post-Structuralist Criticism,* ed. Josué V. Harari (Ithaca: Cornell Univ. Press, 1979), pp. 82-120.

32. Here I use, and am indebted to, Lanham's important distinctions. See note 7, above.

Chapter Three

1. For recent illuminating discussions of Pope's possible institutional positions, see Chester Chapin, "Alexander Pope: Eras-

mian Catholic," *Eighteenth-Century Studies,* 6 (1973), 411-30, and Gloria Stevens, "The Question of Consistency in Pope's Religious Thought," Diss. Kansas 1979. My interests, at least, are (as Giles Gunn writes in quite another context) with religion "less as a system of creedal affirmations or a body of dogma than as a mode of experience, a view of life, an imaginative circuit of belief and desire" (*The Interpretation of Otherness: Literature, Religion, and the American Imagination* [New York: Oxford Univ. Press, 1979], p. 111).

2. Herbert N. Schneidau, *Sacred Discontent: The Bible and Western Tradition* (Baton Rouge: Louisiana State Univ. Press, 1976), p. 223.

3. Ibid., p. 99.

4. Ibid., p. 292.

5. Ibid., p. 141.

6. Schneidau makes this point (*Sacred Discontent,* pp. 48-49n.).

7. Ibid., p. 292.

8. Reb Derissa is a name used by Derrida, a Sephardic Jew, who writes much about "the people of the Book." See, for example, "Edmond Jabès and the Question of the Book" and "Ellipsis," in *Writing and Difference,* trans. Alan Bass (Chicago: Univ. of Chicago Press, 1978), and Susan A. Handelman, *The Slayers of Moses: The Emergence of Rabbinic Interpretation in Modern Literary Theory* (Albany: State Univ. of New York Press, 1982).

9. Schneidau, *Sacred Discontent,* pp. 16-17.

10. Ibid., p. 64.

11. Murray Krieger, "'Trying Experiments upon Our Sensibility': The Art of Dogma and Doubt in Eighteenth-Century Literature," in *Poetic Presence and Illusion: Essays in Critical History and Theory* (Baltimore: Johns Hopkins Univ. Press, 1980), p. 80.

12. Ibid., p. 81.

13. Schneidau, *Sacred Discontent,* p. 49.

14. J. Hillis Miller, "The Critic as Host," in Bloom et al., *Deconstruction and Criticism,* pp. 217-53.

15. See, esp., Voegelin's monumental study, *Order and History* (Baton Rouge: Louisiana State Univ. Press, 1956-).

16. See, for example, 1.266, 2.282, 3.98, 4.193, as well as the discussion of this metaphor in Aubrey Williams, *Pope's "Dunciad."*

17. See, for example, William Sherlock, *A Discourse Concerning the Divine Providence* (London, 1694), and a whole array of tracts by divines and others, including Henry Fielding. See also the recent work of Aubrey Williams and other members of the so-called Providentialist School, including Williams's *An Approach to Congreve* (New Haven: Yale Univ. Press, 1979).

18. René Girard quotes Ulysses' speech and analyzes social differentiation in *Violence and the Sacred*, trans. Patrick Gregory (Baltimore: Johns Hopkins Univ. Press, 1977), pp. 50-51.

19. Maynard Mack, *"King Lear" in Our Time* (Berkeley: Univ. of California Press, 1965), p. 111.

20. Note the use twice in this passage of the verb "supply," which carries a double meaning akin to that of *supplément*.

21. Maynard Mack, in his notes to the poem in the edition used throughout (Vol. III.i). See also the helpful discussion by Douglas H. White, *Pope and the Context of Controversy: The Manipulation of Ideas in "An Essay on Man"* (Chicago: Univ. of Chicago Press, 1970), esp. pp. 19-40.

22. The terms "proper" (i.e., one's own), "property" (what is one's own, what one owns), "propriation," "propriety," "appropriate" are, of course, all closely linked, a fact that Derrida does not fail to exploit as he undermines the notion of *propre*. As Geoffrey Hartman has written, in Derrida "all properties are questioned until the *propre* itself . . . comes into question" (*Saving the Text*, p. 93). Indeed, deconstruction might even be defined (if definitions were possible) as an attempt to subvert the notion of the "proper," on which Western thinking appears to rest. The idea of the "proper" connotes a perhaps ineradicable desire of presence, of being in place, of having a single, definite, and distinct identity. But, writes Derrida in *Of Grammatology*, treating that most proper of the proper, the proper noun, "When within *consciousness*, the name is *called* proper, it is already classified and is obliterated in *being named*. It is already no more than a *so-called* proper name" (p. 109). Discussing, and deconstructing, Lévi-Strauss's experiences among the Nambikwara,

Derrida continues: "To name, to give names that it will on occasion be forbidden to pronounce, such is the originary violence of language which consists in inscribing within a difference, in classifying, in suspending the vocative absolute. To think the unique *within* the system, to inscribe it there, such is the gesture of the arche-writing: arche-violence, loss of the proper, of absolute proximity, of self-presence, in truth the loss of what has never taken place, of a self-presence which has never been given but only dreamed of and always already split, repeated, incapable of appearing to itself except in its own disappearance" (p. 112). Contrary, then, to our prevailing assumption, Derrida claims, the "proper" has never been proper. As Hartman puts it, "The *nom propre* is *non-propre*" (*Saving the Text*, p. 59).

23. John Dominic Crossan, "Difference and Divinity," in *Derrida and Biblical Studies*, ed. Robert Detweiler, an issue of *Semeia: An Experimental Journal for Biblical Criticism*, 23 (1982), 33.

24. See ibid., p. 34.

25. Martin Price has helpfully discussed the self-difference of *An Essay on Man* in his *To the Palace of Wisdom: Studies in Order and Energy from Dryden to Blake* (New York: Doubleday, 1964). For Price, the "central contradictions of Pope's *Essay* lie in the conflict between an aesthetic vision and a moral one" (p. 142).

Chapter Four

1. Miriam Leranbaum, *Alexander Pope's 'Opus Magnum' 1729-1744* (Oxford: Clarendon Press, 1977).

2. Pope himself wrote that his "works will in one respect be like the works of Nature, much more to be liked and understood when consider'd in the relation they bear with each other, than when ignorantly look'd upon one by one" (*Correspondence* III, 348). For recent attempts to stress such relations among Pope's poems, see Ralph Cohen, "Pope's Meanings and the Strategies of Interpretation," in *English Literature in the Age of Disguise*, ed. Maximillian E. Novak (Berkeley: Univ. of California Press,

1977), and Wallace Jackson, *Vision and Re-Vision in Alexander Pope* (Detroit: Wayne State Univ. Press, 1983).

3. *Burlington* was published in December 1731, *To Bathurst* in January 1733, *To Cobham* in January 1734, and *To a Lady* in February 1735. Pope brought the four together in the 1735 edition of his *Works*, giving them the order now universally adopted: *Cobham, To a Lady, Bathurst,* and *Burlington.* See Leranbaum, *Alexander Pope's 'Opus Magnum' 1729–1744* and III.ii (*Epistles to Several Persons*) in the Twickenham Edition of the *Poems.*

4. For a recent consideration of interpretation as a major concern in the *Moral Essays*, see Fredric V. Bogel, *Acts of Knowledge: Pope's Later Poems* (Lewisburg, Penn.: Bucknell Univ. Press, 1981). See also Max Byrd, "'Reading' in *Great Expectations*," *PMLA*, 91 (1976), 259-65.

5. On this point, cf. the different positions of James R. Kincaid, "Coherent Readers, Incoherent Texts," *Critical Inquiry*, 3 (1977), 781-802, and John Dominic Crossan, e.g., *Raid on the Articulate: Comic Eschatology in Jesus and Borges* (New York: Harper and Row, 1976), p. 44.

6. For detailed discussion of the ruling passion and its background, see Douglas H. White, *Pope and the Context of Controversy: The Manipulation of Ideas in "An Essay on Man"* (Chicago: Univ. of Chicago Press, 1970), esp. pp. 144-72.

7. Whereas Derrida writes that woman "plays at dissimulation, at ornamentation, deceit, artifice . . . " (*Spurs: Nietzsche's Styles*, trans. Barbara Harlow [Chicago: Univ. of Chicago Press, 1978], p. 67), Pope declares, "Ladies, like variegated Tulips, show, / 'Tis to their Changes that their charms they owe" (ll. 41-42). And just as Pope writes that "by submitting [woman] sways" (l. 263), so Derrida declares: "Either, at times, woman is woman because she gives, *because she gives* herself, while the man for his part takes, possesses, indeed takes possession. Or else, at other times, she is woman because, in giving, she is in fact *giving herself for*, is simulating, and consequently assuring the possessive mastery for her own self" (p. 109). Further, Derrida claims that "There is no such thing as a woman, as a truth

in itself of woman in itself" (p. 101), Pope's parallel position being that "Woman's at best a Contradiction still" (l. 270).

8. See *Literature and Psychoanalysis: The Question of Reading: Otherwise*, ed. Shoshana Felman (Baltimore: Johns Hopkins Univ. Press, 1982), e.g., pp. 2-10. This collection of essays originally appeared as *Yale French Studies*, nos. 55-56.

9. Derrida, *Positions*, pp. 41-42. As Derrida makes clear, and I noted earlier, the temporal language is misleading since "it is not a question of a chronological phase, a given moment, or a page that one day simply will be turned, in order to go onto other things" (ibid.).

10. I have in mind here Derrida's sense of truth as woman as well as the historical emergence of a quasi-liberated woman on the seventeenth-century English stage. See Jean Gagen, *The Emergence of the New Woman* (New York: Twayne, 1954), and Culler, *On Deconstruction*, esp. pp. 43-64.

11. de Man, *Allegories of Reading*, p. 12.

12. See Culler, *On Deconstruction*, esp. pp. 64-83. See also Kincaid, "Coherent Readers, Incoherent Texts."

13. Helpful critical studies include Wasserman, *Pope's "Epistle to Bathurst"*; Keener, *An Essay on Pope*; Leranbaum, *Alexander Pope's 'Opus Magnum' 1729-1744*; Bogel, *Acts of Knowledge*; and Jackson, *Vision and Re-Vision in Alexander Pope*.

14. Marc Shell, *The Economy of Literature* (Baltimore: Johns Hopkins Univ. Press, 1978) and *Money, Language, and Thought: Literary and Philosophical Economies from the Medieval to the Modern Era* (Berkeley: Univ. of California Press, 1982). See also my forthcoming essay "The Money of Stories of Money."

15. Cf. Shell's account of Heidegger's similar hope for "a barter or premonetary (pre-Heraclitean) economy of words as well as wares" (*Money, Language, and Thought*, p. 174).

16. See, esp., Shell's chapter "The Gold Bug" in *Money, Language, and Thought*, pp. 5-23.

17. Shell, *Economy of Literature*, p. 34.

18. This last point was suggested by Shell (*Economy of Liter-*

ature, p. 40). Note the following remark by Michel Foucault: "the signs of exchange, because they satisfy desire, are sustained by the dark, dangerous, and accursed glitter of metal. An equivocal glitter, for it reproduces in the depths of the earth that other glitter that sings at the far end of the night: it resides there like an inverted promise of happiness, and, because metal resembles the stars, the knowledge of all these perilous treasures is at the same time knowledge of the world. And thus reflection upon wealth has its pivot in the broadest speculation upon the cosmos, just as, inversely, profound knowledge of the order of the world must lead to the secret of metals and the possession of wealth" (*The Order of Things: An Archaeology of the Human Sciences* [New York: Vintage, 1970], p. 173).

19. For a helpful discussion of the relation of light to being, see Williams, *Pope's "Dunciad*," p. 140. On the relation of truth to the sun, see Derrida, "White Mythology: Metaphor in the Text of Philosophy," in *Margins of Philosophy*, pp. 207-71.

20. Shell, *Economy of Literature*, p. 62.

21. de Man, *Allegories of Reading*, pp. 3-19.

22. Wasserman, *Pope's "Epistle to Bathurst*," p. 31.

23. A point also made by Shell (*Economy of Literature*, p. 105).

24. Pope's own notation to l. 250.

25. See Mack, *"King Lear" in Our Time*, p. 111.

26. Johnson, "Translator's Introduction" to Derrida, *Dissemination*, p. xiii.

27. Derrida, "Differance," pp. 133-34.

28. Ibid., p. 132.

29. In a provocative account claiming that Pope is more interested in ways of interpreting the world than in any interpretation of it, Bogel argues that *Bathurst* casts its lot with *process* (*Acts of Knowledge*, esp. pp. 37-107).

Chapter Five

1. Among the most illuminating of these studies are Robert W. Rogers, *The Major Satires of Alexander Pope*, Illinois Studies

in Lang. and Lit. 40 (Urbana, 1952); Reuben A. Brower, *Alexander Pope: The Poetry of Allusion* (Oxford: Clarendon Press, 1959); Thomas E. Maresca, *Pope's Horatian Poems* (Columbus: Ohio State Univ. Press, 1966); Peter Dixon, *The World of Pope's Satires* (London: Methuen, 1968); John M. Aden, *Something like Horace: Studies in the Art and Allusion of Pope's Horatian Satires* (Nashville: Vanderbilt Univ. Press, 1969); Griffin, *Alexander Pope: The Poet in the Poems;* and Howard D. Weinbrot, *Augustus Caesar in "Augustan England": The Decline of a Classical Norm* (Princeton: Princeton Univ. Press, 1978) and *Alexander Pope and the Traditions of Formal Verse Satire* (Princeton: Princeton Univ. Press, 1982).

2. See, for example, Brower, *Alexander Pope,* and Leonard Moskovit, "Pope's Purposes in *Sober Advice,*" *Philological Quarterly,* 44 (1965), 195-99.

3. Maynard Mack, *The Garden and the City: Retirement and Politics in the Later Poetry of Pope, 1731-43* (Toronto: Univ. of Toronto Press, 1969).

4. See my "Strategy and Purpose in Pope's *Sober Advice from Horace,*" *Papers on Language and Literature,* 15 (1978), 159-74.

5. See, for example, the note by "Bentley" to line 36 in the Latin poem: "CUNNI CUPIENNIUS ALBI, *Hoary Shrine.* Here the Imitator grievously errs, *Cunnus albus* by no means signifying a *white* or *grey Thing,* but a Thing under a *white* or *grey Garment,* which thing may be either black, brown, red, or parti-coloured."

6. See, for example, *Epilogue to the Satires,* Dialogue I.228-47.

7. René Girard, "The Plague in Literature and Myth," in *"To Double Business Bound"* (Baltimore: Johns Hopkins Univ. Press, 1978), p. 138.

8. Cf. *Epilogue to the Satires,* Dialogue II.212-19.

9. Cf. Stanley Fish's somewhat simpler view that irony is "neither the property of works, nor the creation of an unfettered imagination, but a way of reading, an interpretive strategy that produces the object of its attention, an object that will be perspicuous to those who share or have been persuaded to share the same strategy" ("Short People Got No Reason to Live: Reading Irony," *Daedalus,* 112 [1983], 189).

10. Irvin Ehrenpreis, *Acts of Implication: Suggestion and Covert Meaning in the Works of Dryden, Swift, Pope and Austen* (Berkeley: Univ. of California Press, 1981), p. 89. On more than one occasion I have tried to read the poem's "speaker" as a coherent *persona*, but, despite the strong desire to simplify, I have not been able to make him consistent.

11. Cf. the doubleness associated with "patron" in *An Epistle to Dr. Arbuthnot*, a point I discuss later in this chapter.

12. Joel Weinsheimer, "'London' and the Fundamental Problem of Hermeneutics," *Critical Inquiry*, 9 (1982), 314.

13. Stephen Booth, *"King Lear," "Macbeth," Indefinition, and Tragedy* (New Haven: Yale Univ. Press, 1983), pp. 85-86.

14. J. Hillis Miller, "Character in the Novel / A 'Real Illusion,'" in *From Smollett to Trollope: Studies in the Novel and Other Essays Presented to Edgar Johnson*, ed. Samuel I. Mintz, Alice Chandler, and Christopher Mulvey (Charlottesville: Univ. Press of Virginia, 1981), p. 279. I wish Miller had placed "speaking" and "voice" in quotation marks, obviating concern about phonocentrism here creeping into his deconstruction.

15. Roland Barthes, "The Death of the Author," in *Image / Music / Text*, trans. Stephen Heath (New York: Hill and Wang, 1977), p. 145.

16. Eduard Fraenkel, *Horace* (Oxford: Clarendon Press, 1957), p. 78.

17. From "Inhibitions, Symptoms and Anxiety," quoted in "Translator's Preface" to Derrida, *Of Grammatology*, p. xlvii.

18. Miller, "The Critic as Host."

19. Derrida, *Spurs*, pp. 49-51.

20. The poem's fictionality is apparent in the way Pope depicts his mother, who died in June 1733, eighteen months before *Arbuthnot* was published.

21. The question of homosexuality is obviously raised by Pope's worry about his masculinity and by the threat posed by *male* writers. This issue may begin to loom large when we note that Pope writes that his friends "left me GAY" (l. 256; *we* at least cannot but hear the slang term in the phrase). But the issue is primarily one of the division within individuals, whereby, as in Chinese philosophy, nothing is purely masculine or purely fem-

inine. As in the treatment of Sporus, Pope's chief concern is with the both/and nature of things, Sporus, for example, *oscillating* between male and female.

22. Maresca, *Pope's Horatian Poems*, p. 71.

23. Aubrey Williams, ed., *Poetry and Prose of Alexander Pope* (Boston: Houghton Mifflin, 1969), p. 207n.

24. Miller, "Critic as Host," p. 221.

25. Ibid.

26. A similar point appears in the "Advertisement" to *The Dunciad Variorum:* "*it is only in this monument that* [the dunces] *must expect to survive.*"

Chapter Six

1. Jackson, *Vision and Re-Vision in Alexander Pope*, p. 148.

2. Williams, *Pope's "Dunciad,"* p. 156. Other valuable studies of the poem include, besides those I mention in my text, Alvin B. Kernan, "*The Dunciad* and the Plot of Satire," *Studies in English Literature*, 2 (1962), 255-66; Emrys Jones, "Pope and Dulness," *Proceedings of the British Academy*, 54 (1968), 231-63; John Sitter, *The Poetry of Pope's "Dunciad"* (Minneapolis: Univ. of Minnesota Press, 1971); and Dustin H. Griffin, *Alexander Pope: The Poet in the Poems*.

3. Williams, *Pope's "Dunciad,"* p. 104.

4. Ibid., pp. 105, 114.

5. Hartman, *Criticism in the Wilderness*, p. 239.

6. Bogel, "Dulness Unbound," p. 846.

7. Atkins, "Pope and Difference," pp. 407-8.

8. Bogel, "Dulness Unbound," p. 845.

9. The concluding phrase in "A Letter to the Publisher," p. 21.

10. Williams, *Pope's "Dunciad,"* p. 114.

11. Ibid., p. 127.

12. Ibid., p. 107.

13. Ibid., p. 158.

14. See, esp., Donald T. Siebert, Jr., "Cibber and Satan: *The Dunciad* and Civilization," *Eighteenth-Century Studies*, 10 (1976-77), 203-21.

15. Williams, *Pope's "Dunciad,"* p. 155. Williams cites Jacques Maritain, *Saint Thomas and the Problem of Evil* (Milwaukee: Marquette Univ. Press, 1942), pp. 1-3.

16. William Kinsley, *"The Dunciad* as Mock-Book," in *Pope: Recent Essays by Several Hands,* p. 723; this essay first appeared in *Huntington Library Quarterly,* 35 (1971), 29-47.

17. Ibid., pp. 726-27.

18. Williams, *Pope's "Dunciad,"* p. 77. A meticulous close reader, Williams sounds deconstructionist when, for example, he writes that at one point "John Dennis commits the very fault he inveighs against" (p. 85n) and when he declares, concerning the *Dunciad Variorum,* "It is always a case of both/and, never a simple either/or" (pp. 75-76).

19. Williams, *Pope's "Dunciad,"* pp. 60-61.

20. See, for example, the 1729 *Dunciad,* 1.126, 1.133, 1.138, 3.272.

21. Kinsley, *"The Dunciad* as Mock-Book," p. 728.

22. See the suggestive discussion of game, play, and "Edenic" and "post-Darwinian" versions of humanism in Lanham, *Literacy and the Survival of Humanism.*

23. Hartman, *Criticism in the Wilderness,* p. 134.

24. See Hugh Kenner, *The Counterfeiters: A Historical Comedy* (1968; rpt. New York: Anchor, 1973).

25. Williams, *Pope's "Dunciad,"* p. 142.

26. Crossan, "Difference and Divinity," p. 34.

27. Derrida, "Differance," p. 130.

28. Schneidau, *Sacred Discontent,* e.g., p. 47.

29. Bogel, "Dulness Unbound," p. 854, n. 8.

30. See my "'Count It All Joy': The Affirmative Nature of Deconstruction." I am at work on an extended study of deconstruction and religion, which seems to follow logically from this volume on Pope.

Index

Abrams, M. H., 13
Addison, Joseph, 124
Ancients and Moderns, 148, 149
Aristotelianism, 57

Bacon, Francis, 21
Barthes, Roland, 10, 127
Bathurst, Allen Lord, 87
Bentley, Richard, 101, 106, 123,
  150, 151, 153, 154, 156, 181
  n.5
Betterton, Thomas, 117
Bible, 98, 128; as different from
  myth, 41, 43–44; and aliena-
  tion, 42; and deconstruction,
  42, 44, 80; and disillusion-
  ment, 43–44; its "sacred dis-
  content," 43, 60
Blount, Martha, 69, 75
Blount, Sir John, 88–94 *passim*
Bogel, Fredric V., 149–50, 166–
  67
Bolingbroke, Henry St. John,
  Viscount, 1, 49
Booth, Barton, 117
Booth, Stephen, 119
Boyle, Richard, Earl of Burling-
  ton, 75

brisure, 45
Brooks, Cleanth, 32–33
Broome, William, 26
Busby, Richard, 151

Christ, 142
Cibber, Colley, 156
Corinthians, Book of, 129
  (quoted)
Crossan, John Dominic, 64, 165
Culler, Jonathan, 32, 33
Curll, Edmund, 160–61

Dante, 109
declaration/description, 6–10,
  67, 113. *See also* Pope, Alex-
  ander, *works by name*
deconstruction: affirmative na-
  ture of, 2, 4; particular ap-
  proach to, 4; misunderstand-
  ings of, 4–5; as reader-
  responsibility, 5, 6; use of tra-
  ditional interpretive proce-
  dures, 5; and author's inten-
  tions, 5–6, 8; and double
  reading, 5–6, 10, 80; insis-
  tence on situatedness, 5–6; as
  both/and process, 6, 9, 10;